COUNTERLIFE

COUNTERLIFE

SLAVERY AFTER RESISTANCE AND SOCIAL DEATH

CHRISTOPHER FREEBURG

Duke University Press *Durham and London* 2021

Printed in the United States of America on acid-free paper ∞
Designed by Courtney Leigh Richardson
Typeset in Warnock Pro by Copperline Book Services

Library of Congress Cataloging-in-Publication Data
Names: Freeburg, Christopher, [date] author.
Title: Counterlife : slavery after resistance and social
death / Christopher Freeburg.
Description: Durham : Duke University Press, 2021. |
Includes bibliographical references and index.
Identifiers: LCCN 2020020338 (print)
LCCN 2020020339 (ebook)
ISBN 9781478010418 (hardcover)
ISBN 9781478011446 (paperback)
ISBN 9781478012962 (ebook)
Subjects: LCSH: Slavery—United States—History. | Slavery—
United States—Sociological aspects. | Slavery in literature.
Classification: LCC E441.F744 2021 (print) | LCC E441 (ebook) |
DDC 306.3/620973—dc23
LC record available at https://lccn.loc.gov/2020020338
LC ebook record available at https://lccn.loc.gov/2020020339

Cover art: Radcliffe Bailey, *Western Currents*, 2012.
Mixed media on canvas. © Radcliffe Bailey. Courtesy
of the artist and Jack Shainman Gallery, New York.

FOR IMANI, BILL, AND JULIA —

you didn't have to . . . I'm very grateful that you did

CONTENTS

ACKNOWLEDGMENTS

I love what I do. Here is a list of people that help me thrive.

Joseph Brown S.J., always—

Ken Warren is a master interlocutor. I hear my own voice the clearest after our conversations. Lauren Berlant has encouraged me to be patient and thoughtful in the face of frustrating enigmas. Erica Edwards, I can't imagine when I'll stop being grateful for your presence and wise counsel. My discussions of slavery scholarship with Vaughn Rasberry, Illya Davis, Quincy Mills, Allyson Hobbs, Radiclani Clytus, William Balan-Gaubert, Yogita Goyal, and Michael Ralph undoubtedly made this book better. Thank you, Bill Brown, for pointing me back to Weber.

When I gave a talk on this material at Vanderbilt University, Dana Nelson's introduction (and hospitality) catapulted me to cloud nine. I'm right back up there every time I remember it. The thoughtfulness of Jen Fleissner, Laura Mielke, Nancy Bentley, Xiomara Santamarina, Michele Elam, Priscilla Wald, Betsy Duquette, and Marlene Daut go beyond what I can return.

When I travel to Harvard University for any reason, John Stauffer makes time to discuss my current work and hand me an armful of interesting books. Bob Levine read parts of the manuscript early on and gave encouraging feedback. Michael Awkward offered promising suggestions on the relationship between Black music and literature. Derrick Spires is an endless reservoir of pertinent references from early African American culture.

At the University of Illinois, Urbana-Champaign, Janice Harrington's appreciation for my ideas helps me courageously step into new ones. Bob Parker's enthusiasm for critical discussion and deep sense of care for me, our department and profession are truly inspirational. Trish Loughran,

Candice Jenkins, and Irving Hunt are repositories of insight and fantastic colleagues. Thank you to my department heads, Vicki Mahaffey and Robert Markley, for their valuable support.

I've had the tremendous opportunity to present selections from this book to faculty, graduate students, and the broader public at the English Departments at Vanderbilt University, Johns Hopkins University, Stanford University, the University of Michigan, and the University of Kansas. Deborah McDowell and the great people at the Carter G. Woodson Institute at the University of Virginia made me feel especially welcome. A special thank-you to everyone who read my work so closely, showed up, and showed out in the very best academic spirit at the ELH colloquium at Johns Hopkins University. I really want to thank Doug Mao, Chris Nealon, Larry Jackson, and Jarvis Young for their thoughtful feedback. Margo Crawford, Dag Woubshet, Charles Rowell, and the *Callaloo* family, thank you for welcoming me with open arms to an incredibly moving conference at the University of Pennsylvania.

Thank you to all the people at Duke University Press. Courtney Berger is the most patient, attentive, and thorough editor I've ever worked with. Thank you, Sandra Korn and Lisl Hampton, for your patience in stewarding this book through. The Editorial Advisory Board at the press offered valuable suggestions.

Having a space of support is crucial to the life of a thinker. Ben Quattrone, thank you for always making space for me to work and eat comfort food at Honda BMW of Champaign.

I'm infinitely grateful for Sarah Morris Jarrett, my mother and muse of the grandest care I can imagine, along with Orville Morris Jarrett, a man not short of a thousand sacrifices. My father, John Freeburg, bless his soul, ceaselessly cheered me on—still does. Grandma Jean Freeburg's love, care, and artistic insight radiate through this work. My beloved Aunt Elmyra Powell, our stories live through you. We can now carry the torch.

My wife, Izabelle, and my children, Brianna and Jonathan, keep me present and in tune with God's love. Jason Stephenson and Terrence Satterfield never let me lose sight of my dreams, "for if dreams die . . ."

INTRODUCTION

Slavery's Hereafter

There may not be a more aspirational word in the modern West than *freedom*. But its sordid twin, *slavery*, furnishes freedom with its starry luster and glowing sentiment. Preeminent historian John Hope Franklin knew this and named the arc of African American life in the United States an epic journey *From Slavery to Freedom* (1947). Sociologist Orlando Patterson's major study of slavery throughout recorded history appeared as a necessary precursor to his equally acclaimed book *Freedom* (1991). Toni Morrison, perhaps the foremost artistic voice on slavery and its aftermath, wrote that "the slave population . . . offered itself up as surrogate selves for meditation on the problems of human freedom."[1] These iconic voices confirm the fundamental entanglement of slavery and freedom. When it comes to making sense of either concept, whether in modernity's edifices or in the ruins of ancient worlds, one rarely finds freedom without slavery or slavery without freedom. If one is missing, the other lies in wait nearby. From Georg W. F. Hegel's description of lordship and bondage to Harriet Jacobs plotting her liberation from a tomb-like crawl space to Nat Turner's violent uprising, slavery and freedom are inseparable.[2]

As 1862 neared its end, President Abraham Lincoln signed the Emancipation Proclamation, which freed most slaves. The Thirteenth Amendment, ratified in 1865, outlawed slavery. Yet what scholars call "the afterlife of slavery" continued to appear in the form of convict leasing, sharecropping, domestic work, and other abhorrent labor practices, in addition to widespread lynching, sexual violence, and political disenfranchisement.[3] Whether scholars are discussing slavery or its afterlife, it typically becomes an opportunity to address freedom achieved, delayed, or obstructed.

When we approach historical or aesthetic representations of slavery, this opposition between slavery and freedom usually defines the lens of discovery.[4] In fact, it is challenging to discuss, even to contemplate, the lives of enslaved Africans or depictions of slaves in art without also addressing how what they are doing and thinking somehow bends toward or away from the arc of freedom—toward or away from acts that disrupt whites in power. The slavery/freedom opposition informs dominant conceptual rubrics—such as agency/power, social death/social life, damage/resistance, and haunting—that scholars have used to guide, explain, and legitimize the importance of slavery research. There is no doubt that these rubrics organize and underscore a wide and rich body of work on slave culture and representations of slavery in modern art. But despite the profundity of nuanced microhistories and theoretical models of what it is to be a slave, scholars have yet to fully address the question this book seeks to answer: can we analyze the depictions of enslaved Africans—which contain physical violence, psychic terror, spiritual deliverance, and artistic genius—without the critical perspectives that emphasize slaves' success or failure to disrupt their masters' control over them?

For instance, "Steal Away" is a beautiful spiritual that was composed and performed by enslaved Africans. The lyrics testify to the singers' spiritual commitment and claim to heaven's kingdom: "My Lord calls me . . . I hain't got long to stay here. Steal away. . . ."[5] While scholars appreciate the rich poetic lyricism and the theological and folkloric sophistication of this spiritual, they repeatedly return to the song's political imprint: by patiently waiting on the Lord, rather than resisting bondage, slaves reinforced the interests of white masters.[6] Other scholars, though, insist the title phrase "Steal Away" and the line "I hain't got long to stay here" reflect a rejection of white dominance because slaves used the song to secretly refer to resisting and escaping slavery.[7] Joseph A. Brown explains that gatherings of enslaved Africans to sing spirituals like "Steal Away" were communal calls to conversion.[8] From this insight, one can draw on the vast records of ex-

slaves' conversion narratives from books such as Clifton H. Johnson's col-
lection *God Struck Me Dead* (1969) or the slave autobiographies John Blassingame put together in *Slave Testimony* (1977) to rethink "Steal Away" in
the context of how slaves thought about being called by God and the challenges of accepting new forms of spiritual identity. Thinking "Steal Away"
as a spiritual and communal activity opens up a different set of questions
and narrative possibilities: Who gathers to sing and why? How did slaves
create and revise their performances to balance the necessities of individual expression with the needs of the group? By addressing "Steal Away"
in this social, performative, and ethnographic sense we can bypass former
rubrics of accommodation and resistance because the inquiry's focus is rediscovering how slaves produced transformative meaning for themselves;
the answers do not necessarily become more or less significant based on
how precisely they can indicate slaves' level of resistance or complicity
with white dominance. Sifting through conversion narratives, accounts of
slaves singing spirituals like "Steal Away," and other slave religious gatherings, we discover daunting yet inspiring possibilities for figuring the meaning slaves produced in their performance of songs.

This idea captures the spirit and method of this book, which is to tarry
in the daunting possibilities of enslaved Africans' lives as they appear in
various artistic texts in the United States from the time of slavery to the
present. This book recommits to the idea that the lives of enslaved Africans are provocatively enigmatic or, as Ralph Ellison puts it, "infinitely
suggestive."[9] Ellison's phrasing lies at the heart of what I call the *counterlife of slavery.*

Counterlife: Slavery after Resistance and Social Death thinks through
and beyond an imperative to examine slave texts for political freedom or
the mining of slaves' thinking for remedies to contemporary racialized collective projects of repair, recovery, and redemption. These very important
critical approaches currently dominate the field, and this book contributes
to a different story in the study of slavery, one that focuses on philosophical, aesthetic, and historical conundrums and contradictions of slavery
without an emphasis on political progress.

This book conceptualizes slave social life and art discourse as *counterlife.* Counterlife unsettles singular narratives, teloses, fixed categories,
oppositions, and what it means to be or have a self. The counterlife of slavery has to do with realizing that slaves' lives, across art and media, exceed
the explanatory force of the terms that currently define the field. Through
the counterlife lens, when slaves acquire philosophical insights, create art,

seize religious meaning, commit acts of violence, or perform historical memory, they prompt simultaneous and multiple points of critical view—a profound irreducibility—which take on their own importance. Reading for counterlife helps us discover how slave texts reveal the "disorderly flux of life" and thinking inside violent oppressive environments to which conventional terms and frames do not fully attend.[10]

The term *counterlife* originates with Philip Roth's novel *The Counterlife* (1986). Roth never defines the term explicitly. Through the lives of its characters the novel challenges readers' expectations about what makes good or normal life. Roth's novel is not just about upending surprises on the course and direction of characters' lives, but it is about a complete undoing of expected conventions. *The Counterlife* has inspired me to make every effort to abandon my expectations when I approach the social lives of slaves in various art and media. Without rediscovering slavery outside the conventional frames and rubrics, we run the risk of treating the intense social frictions that slave texts capture as "life proof"—what Roth calls "well-prepared discourse, . . . cunningly selected, self-protecting words."[11] *Counterlife* is my signal to experiment with abandoning these rubrics and trajectories.[12] In doing so, this book is my way to revisit slavery's sociality and its artistic representations. I deploy *counterlife* to realize profound instability and mystery anew in the relations among Black social life, artistic expression, and oppressive institutions. The counterlife of slavery, then, is my call to be vulnerable to what is undoubtedly enigmatic and irreducible in slave texts—to bear witness to the force of slavery's artistic representations without measuring their importance on scales of political efficacy.

Breaking through frames, rubrics, and normative conventions is certainly not original to Roth. The relentless self-questioning and unmaking of heavily choreographed racial prescriptions occurs throughout modern Black texts, such as Ralph Ellison's *Invisible Man* (1952). Like Ellison, James Baldwin repeatedly railed against using familiar categories, frames, and stereotypes for insight into slavery and modern Black life because the familiar served only to protect us from the social and psychological chaos we find most challenging to grasp. Baldwin argues that we use the clarity of categorical thinking to fend off the parts of life that are multifaceted, unstable, and above all intractable.[13] Trey Ellis called for a "new black aesthetic" at the dawn of the 1990s that rejected the moral imperatives of Black Nationalist art. For Ellis the new Black aesthetic required no imperative beyond proclaiming that "anything goes."[14] Even more recently, when Thelma Golden put together innovative exhibits with Glenn Ligon, her effort was "to think outside existing paradigms" for contemporary Black art practices. Ligon and Golden used *post-black* to describe their efforts to unburden Black artists' installations from previous Black aesthetic movements.[15] From Baldwin's rejection of neat categorizations to Ligon's and Golden's post-Black aesthetic curations for art galleries and museums, Black artists have found a rhetoric and practice of both bearing a Black tradition and harnessing the courage to reinvent it.

I deploy *counterlife* in this book as a way to galvanize radical imperatives—thus, I draw on the transformative currents offered by art curators like Golden, visual artists like Mark Bradford and Radcliffe Bailey, and writers like Ellis, Baldwin, and Ellison. I find counterlife liberating as a theoretical point of departure because I use the concept to call on a constellation of irreverent and rambunctious thinkers to return to the slave archive as a way to bear witness to how slaves repeatedly outstrip the labels and the horizons we've orchestrated for them.[16]

This book is certainly not the first to claim that the way we discuss slavery is too prescriptive. Critics have a recurring preoccupation with addressing the long-standing limitations of slavery studies. In fact, there is no generation of scholars since the 1950s that has not imagined itself as outstripping narrow "either/or" categories and dialectics that hauntingly recur. Decades ago, Herbert Gutman said it best: scholars have "encased" slave life in "snug and static ahistorical opposites."[17] More recent work by historians such as Stephanie Camp and Edward Baptist insists that other scholars push beyond "accommodation/resistance" as way to evaluate slaves' social life. Piggybacking off Camp and Baptist, Walter Johnson critiques the ever-present sliding scale between *agency* and *power*.[18] In addition to the former historians, art historian Darby English claims that when scholars approach contemporary art exhibitions that feature slavery, such as those of Ligon and Kara Walker, they focus on evidence of Black resistance. English sees current conversations about these artists' exhibits as constrained by "dynamic oppositional entanglements" rooted in Black politics.[19]

In anthropology, David Scott argues that studies of colonialism and slavery tend to be written as agential narratives of overcoming and vindication—"stories of salvation and redemption."[20] Literary and cultural critic Stephen Best sees in Black studies a conflict between two modes of inquiry: critics seeing their own agency vested in the recovery of enslaved Africans' "political agency," and a "melancholy historicism" that sees the articulation of slave subjectivity as constituted by white dominance's refusals of it.[21] These scholars register the persistent problem of an oppositional framing that stakes its significance on political outcomes or calls attention to the shadowy guise of Black freedom's unrealized horizon.

One important way Scott claims to get beyond romantic dyads of political triumph and disappointment is to analyze slavery's artifacts, texts, and conflicts in terms of tragedy. The tragic, as Scott renders it, focuses on "unstable and ambiguous" aspects of historical conflict and events and takes human action as "ever open to unaccountable contingencies."[22] I am fully sympathetic to Scott's encouragement to move scholarship beyond the failures and successes of romantic horizons, but he prompts a more direct rendering of a conundrum that continues to challenge us. Most cultural critics of slavery would argue that they address slave social life as unsettled and ambiguous already. I can think of almost no critic or thinker who believes they fail to see complexity and ambiguity.

For instance, Daphne Brooks analyzes slave texts for "ruptures and blind spots where . . . performers defy expectations and desires," and as such, Brooks zeroes in on "fraught and volatile dynamics" between self and other, audience and performer.[23] In a similar vein with a different focus, Uri McMillan explains how slave texts speak back to and disrupt objectifying forces.[24] Both McMillan and Brooks pointedly attend to the nuances, vicissitudes, and ambiguities of Black performances' entanglement with abjection. What I am struck by in McMillan's examination of "multiple identifications and hoaxes" in slave texts is how he grounds his claims squarely within the presence and import of "subjectivity and agency."[25] Brooks's study of dialectics between performers and audiences also draws its salience from finding a "bridge out of abjection."[26]

Brooks's and McMillan's crucial work is not diminished by this emphasis on how Black subjects express subjectivity, demonstrate agency, and forge pathways through abjection. Yet their work does prompt me to ask how we can discuss what is radical about slave texts without bracketing such texts in critical conventions such as "subjectivity and agency" or escapes from abjection. Can we have a commitment to oppositional categories as definitive framing devices and also see the very slave texts within those frames as *beyond* boundaries? When it comes to rubrics, frames, and overall emphases, the critical tradition around slavery seems to want to have its cake and eat it too: slave texts capture the unbridled force of instability and improvisation that transcends our forms and modes of thinking; yet, we hold on dearly to rubrics that frame how we approach slave texts. This book takes its cue from scholars who seek to transform the immediate "political-imperative" of a "black political present" but also take seriously the idea of Black radical imagination(s).[27] In order to do this, we need to heed more faithfully Michel-Rolph Trouillot's call to "change the terms of the debate."[28]

Counterlife builds on the work of Brooks, Scott, McMillan, Best, and others to enrich further our understanding of slaves' experiences and performances across texts and media. My readings deprioritize political transformation as a goal in and of itself and instead focus on how slaves establish religious practices, recall and perform historical memory, and find personal meaning in artistic creation. Slave texts also offer a crucial opportunity to witness the wide-ranging duality and multiplicity of life perspectives in the most degrading and hostile of conditions.[29] I look to films, television cartoons, literature, and slave music to demonstrate that their aesthetic and philosophical legitimacy does not need to be assessed in relation to political utility. Rediscovering enslaved Africans through counterlife gives us an opportunity as scholars to push in new directions. This book's pages stretch, deform, and reimagine how we approach slavery by reveling in the unsettling and troubling force I identify across a myriad of texts and media.[30]

Through a rich array of cultural forms—literature, music, comedy sketches, and film—*Counterlife* deepens and broadens how we view portrayals of enslaved Africans in the United States. This book's archival tapestry draws from artistic episodes both real and imagined. There are many reasons—ethical, political, and methodological—for distinguishing between actual enslaved Africans' experiences and artists' portrayals of enslaved Africans, but this book is most interested in shifting the terms critics use to frame and analyze representations of slavery. Hence, a contemporary film such as Quentin Tarantino's *Django Unchained* (2012), Toni Morrison's novel *Beloved* (1987), and performed spirituals such as "Go Down, Moses," all get treated similarly as opportunities to get us beyond oppositional rubrics. I use *counterlife* as a rubric to mine paradigmatic slave texts (by or about slaves), from slave narratives to spirituals to cartoons to film, for moments when I can raise and highlight the importance of how slaves seek, find, and lose meaning in their own spiritual affirmation, philosophical conundrums, and artistic creativity. I examine the tropes, beliefs, and strategies for interpreting social reality that for decades constituted the terrain for discussions of slavery.

What is more, *Counterlife* answers these crucial yet often overlooked scholarly questions: What role did debates between artists and social scientists concerning aesthetic form and modern Black life play in these definitive early years of slavery scholarship? How did scholars imagine the plantation spatially, geographically, and culturally when they debated the degree to which slaves were damaged or capable of resistance? I submit that debates about modern Black social reality from the 1930s to the 1960s— when artists like Baldwin and Ellison were especially influential—had a major impact on how scholars have imagined and still imagine the conditions of slaves. Ellison and other artists focused on the irreducible capacity of how people think and live within the confines of formidable institutions. I turn this aesthetic and social insight into a philosophical emphasis on psychological and social irreducibility that thinks through slave texts across a variety of works and periods.

In the first chapter, "Sambo's Cloak," I continue my interest in loosening the more rigid rubrics that shape discussions of slavery by thinking about the ungraspable aspects of personal expression that reveal themselves in social conflict. To this end, I begin with a salient moment from the last century that gives historical and conceptual texture to how discussing slavery in terms of power and agency began and why it is important now to explore and demonstrate alternative points of view. In this chapter I identify Stanley Elkins's book *Slavery* (1959) as a historical prism through which we can see how debates by artists and social scientists about modern space, mass culture, and socialization impacted critics' portrayals of Black social relations. Elkins's infamous book inspired fierce debate in Black cultural studies for decades and helped to crystallize oppositional frames like resistance/damage and agency/power. But what I demonstrate in this historical chapter is Elkins's ongoing impact: how his techniques of re-creating the antebellum plantation, which appear outdated to us, produced a critical *slavery aesthetic* that remains with us. Elkins's contribution, then, is not just polemical and dialectical, as we may understand, but seminal in the way he influenced how we imagine slave social life.

"Kaleidoscope Views," chapter 2, reads crucial moments in Frederick Douglass's *Narrative* (1845, 1855), Edward Jones's *The Known World* (2003), and Radcliffe Bailey's art installations (2007–18) for instances of counterlife. I locate a critique of aesthetic and sociological norms in the work of Douglass and recent art by Jones and Bailey. This section examines Douglass's *Narrative* to see how Douglass uses his relationship to his friend Sandy's conjuring practices to obscure his own cultural knowledge and clarify his moral commitments. Likewise, in Jones's *Known World* the character of Alice seems crafted as a nightmare of social theory, a vessel of comprehensive geography and historical detail, yet at the same time a complete enigma as a free person and slave. Bailey's art installations that feature slavery show mixtures of styles, medium, and materials and a capacious subject that exceeds all logics of time, space, and memory. Like Alice, Bailey's embrace of the materiality of specific historical concepts and events illustrates the tragic power of slavery, yet it contains a seemingly infinite combination of subject positions that elude traditional designations. Douglass, Jones, and Bailey demonstrate key aspects of counterlife: the more we uncover the myriad ways to conceptualize the slave, the more we realize that slave life points to the elusiveness of personhood altogether. I flesh out how these artists signal and unmake established norms for depicting slave social life and use them to define and deepen our understanding of counterlife.

In "Sounds of Blackness," chapter 3, I begin with a basic question: when enslaved Africans sang spirituals, what were they saying, what did it mean, and why is it important? Spirituals demonstrate a commitment to biblical themes, spiritual deliverance, and musical performance, yet their meaning can be elusive. On one hand, scholars claim that the songs reveal slave opposition to their masters; on the other hand, slave singing can be read as making slaves more fit for labor. While such debates have been definitive and important, this chapter addresses neither of these positions. Instead, I focus on the sense of irreconcilable contradiction at the heart of spirituals: the tensions between group history, belief, and tradition and spontaneous, improvisational, and individual differences. By examining slaves' performances in the writings of Douglass, Frederick Law Olmsted, Thomas Wentworth Higginson, W. E. B. Du Bois, and Zora Neale Hurston, as well as in video performances of Aretha Franklin and lesser-known singing and praying bands, I show how tradition can be remembered and kept but also defined by ungraspable dynamism. I advance that irreconcilable contradiction defines the counterlife that spirituals make available—a sense of vibrant mutuality that makes subject/object distinctions unreliable. My goal is to use this sense of conflict to thwart the subject/object debates that critics rely on when they discuss spirituals and other types of Black musical performance. My claim is that "thingness" is a viable lens to engage the sense of contradiction in spiritual slave performances even though thing/subject/object designations do not sufficiently depict what it means to be a slave.[31]

Part of the import of slaves singing spirituals stems from slaves' desire to embody, perform, and redefine their own sense of history; spirituals often contain their own counterhistories. Fiction, film, and cartoons also have been a crucial source for histories that counter racism and images of degraded enslaved Africans. In the final chapter, "The Last Black Hero," I turn to fictional exemplars of iconic Black male heroism. I examine Douglass's novella *The Heroic Slave* (1852), Tarantino's *Django Unchained* (2012), and an episode of Aaron McGruder's *Boondocks* cartoon, "The Story of Catcher Freeman" (2008). These artists all deploy history as countertext— and masculine heroic romances as counterhistory. Counterhistory is also a crucial rubric for slavery scholars looking to redress inaccuracies in the archives of slavery and the absence of the voices and contributions of enslaved Africans. Counterhistories often aim to retell the past with new information and perspectives in the hope to inspire and reform social life and political acts in the present. I argue in this chapter that counterhistory as an aesthetic genre is committed more to the form of storytelling than to history, and as much as heroic romances rely on gendered, stable categories (e.g., good/evil), moral clarity, and predictable emotions, they also reflect the dissonance and unpredictability in social relations. This instability initiates alternative narratives of counterlife in lesser figures in the art that are equally crucial yet void of mythic and heroic qualities. Their stories threaten the cogency and necessity of the heroic counterhistory. What is more, I examine how the masculine heroic form of romance actually expresses what is troubling to people about formlessness, what we fear about an ongoing sense of chaotic uncertainty that is always available in social life—one that makes all subjects unexpectedly subject to one another.

While some critics and artists ponder various counterhistories and counternarratives, others think the United States has a more fundamental problem with slavery. Critics commonly refer to the United States as haunted by slavery; as a country, we repress slavery and do so at a great cost to truth and reconciliation with our nation's past. Given the proliferation of texts, websites, discussion boards, and institutional resources for the study and publication of works on the topic of slavery, does slavery still haunt us? The coda of the book, "Chasing Ghosts," addresses this seemingly never-ending question.

Pheoby's Redress

In writing this book, I found it difficult to escape the terms that have defined much of slavery studies as a field. Here I want to linger a little longer with the challenges of thinking through and beyond the conceptual dyads that grip how we talk about slavery and its residue. Zora Neale Hurston's *Their Eyes Were Watching God* (1937) contains a key figure that gets little attention. Janie, the novel's protagonist, tells her entire story to Pheoby Watson. What kind of listener does Pheoby need to be in order to absorb, understand, and learn from Janie's rich and contradictory experiences? Thinking seriously about what Pheoby offers as a patient and open listener can help us approach counterlife in slave texts.

More recently, scholars and activists have taken quite seriously the idea of listening to texts and people more attentively. Asha Bandele, Tina Campt, and David Scott's conceptions of listening are all instructive for helping us get beyond the impasse of insurgent resistance or slavery's endless residues. For example, in her book *When They Call You a Terrorist* (2018) Bandele explains that community members need to demonstrate better care for one another through listening. When discussing her book at a public library, Bandele was asked to "speak to what it meant . . . to tell this amazing story."[32] Bandele responded: "The deep and abiding lesson was about doing something we do far too little of these days and that's actual deep listening and being present to someone."[33] Scott takes listening as pivotal for revision and new approaches to critical expression. In his meditation on Stuart Hall, he proposes an ethics of listening as a pathway toward considering the more contingent and unsettling aspects of social life. Scott's "listening self" addresses the unpredictability of the world and endeavors to cultivate an "ethos of self-revision and recurrent readjustment to its possibilities."[34] This revision and readjustment relies on being "receptively present to others."[35] In her critical work, Campt uses the idea of "listening to images" as a way to find a "deeper engagement with forgotten histories and suppressed forms of diasporic memories."[36] Campt refashions listening as a way to challenge and expand "what constitutes sound and sonic perception."[37] Campt's formulation insists on a patient engagement with art texts that challenge our initial reactions and critical practices. Bandele, Scott, and Campt all offer their version of listening as a mode of entering into a greater sense of depth, thoughtfulness, attentiveness— a calm fortitude that is intent on moving past initial impressions.

What sets Pheoby apart as a listener in *Their Eyes*? Pheoby is part of the community, but Janie sees the community as largely not interested in her beyond an object to be judged, discussed, and giggled about like an estranged scapegoat that they secretly envy. Pheoby does not objectify Janie and instead connects with her through caring and empathetic intensity. Pheoby does not unfairly judge what Janie has gone through but instead listens to her attentively. Hurston writes: Pheoby is "eager to feel and do through Janie."[38]

Pheoby listens as Janie explains how she felt nourished by her grandmother Nanny's love but was ultimately constrained by Nanny's influence and the trauma of the slave past she embodies. Nanny tells Janie about the violent abuse and coercion she experienced as a slave and also recounts how her daughter, Janie's mother, was raped and tortured after emancipation. Even after emancipation, historian Sarah Haley explains, the rape of Black women continued to reduce "black female bodies to objects of violation and therefore reinforced their social position as flesh, rather than persons."[39] The weight of Black women's bondage and freedom explains why Nanny insists that Janie marry her first suitor, Logan Killicks, as a form of protection. Her marriage to a man she doesn't love and who sees her silence and arduous labor as key to their partnership reveals how her own choice (or the illusion of it) effaces the subject she is and wants to be. In trying to avoid the precarity of the slave past, Janie tragically ends up being treated like Killicks's voiceless mule. Janie detests what her Nanny embodies: enslavement's weighty residue and the violent oppressive social reality that Janie cannot escape.

The most celebrated part of the book, however, is not the reality of slavery's power in Janie's unfreedom but when Hurston's protagonist finds her inner voice, desire, and volition and chooses Teacake. Janie and Teacake choose a new community in the Florida Everglades where they can love, converse, and labor. Here, we witness something akin to freedom for Janie: voice, choice, and agency register powerfully against the brutal regime Nanny survived, yet Janie's agential conquest cannot displace all forms of power. Thus, Janie is both agent and clearly subject to encroaching social constraints—although these are limitations of Janie's choosing along with the freedoms and validation she celebrates.

This is the tug-of-war that one can easily recognize in current critical terms. How can Janie resist, overcome, and transform racist, sexist, and patriarchal structures? Does her sometimes-abusive relationship with Teacake reveal the inescapability of her encroaching past? One could informatively and interestingly rewrite this scenario in a variety of ways, but we still end up weighing the scales of agency and power. What is more, nature, as an environmental, historical, biological, and social force, indubitably shapes Janie. One can read Janie's love for Teacake as a final blossoming, like the vibrant pear tree at the beginning of the novel, her embodiment of sexual longing that becomes as existential and unavoidable as birth and death. Her development is an unstoppable force that entangles social life and biological fact. Hence, Janie is both agent and powerless, victim and victor, existentially cornered yet evidencing the power of choice. There is no way to attribute Janie's being to slavery or its afterlife or what inspires her agential voice overall. The novel speaks so powerfully beyond these oppositional questions.

Pheoby's task as a listener is not to contemplate whether Janie achieves true freedom or the right kind of unfreedom but rather to observe and accept the manifold layers of Janie's experience as a historical subject; slavery, its afterlife, nature, and her inner voice collude and conflict. Pheoby is unsettled and energized by Janie's story. "Ah done growed ten feet higher from jus' listenin' tuh you, Janie. Ah ain't satisfied wid mahself no mo."[40] Pheoby embodies our ideal capacity for receptive listening. She is the receptive listener I hope to emulate in this book. Pheoby empowers Janie as she relays the mutuality, intimacy, and obfuscation between persons. Pheoby is a hungry, curious, and humble listener who may be after the gems of gossip that draw us into the immediacy of storytelling, but she also shows us something to be gained by being patient with the profound enigmas Janie offers.

Approaching slave texts without insisting on political utility is akin to listening like Pheoby, with the realization that a lack of a compelling sense of redress or code of revolution does not diminish the profundity of slave texts. In conceptualizing counterlife throughout this book, I address slave texts aesthetically and philosophically and slaves' experiences as assemblages, amalgams of positions and perspectives that do not have a dogmatic thump of life or death, slavery or freedom but help clear the dead brush away from old pathways for new knowledges and points of view.

1

SAMBO'S CLOAK

The bigger the material mass, the more easily it entraps us.
—Michel-Rolph Trouillot, *Silencing the Past*

For decades, scholars debated one another with different readings from Atlantic slavery's archives. These efforts, while informative, have largely sustained the status quo in terms of frames and rubrics—so much so that scholars appear "locked together in a timeless battle," a "thrust and counterthrust" over the same aporia that resurfaces under different guises: what is the sine qua non of slaves' lives and experiences?[1] In what follows, I shift the focus away from identifying enslaved Africans' elusive experiential essences or their paradigmatic disruptions or their tragic lapses in oppositional consciousness in order to unearth an object hidden beneath the sediment of slavery studies. There is an imaginative field, a hovering *slavery aesthetic*, that reflects the changing same in our scholarly disagreements. In what follows, I raise this slavery aesthetic into full view in order to depict counterlife with greater depth and clarity in the remaining chapters of this book.

I begin with two recent discussions of Toni Morrison's *Beloved* (1987): one, an interview with Angela Davis just after Morrison's passing, and the other, Stephen Best's rendering of recent approaches to slavery's archives in the wake of *Beloved*'s publication. Shortly after Morrison's passing, *Democracy Now* interviewed Angela Davis, Nikki Giovanni, and Sonia Sanchez. Davis's remarks stood out with particular relevance. Davis pondered the unforeseen impact Morrison's *Beloved* had on the way she thought about enslaved Africans: "I think back to the way in which I imagined slavery before reading *Beloved*, and I realized how abstract that imagination was. She taught us, I think probably for the very first time, to imagine enslaved women and men with full lives, with complex subjectivity, with interiority."[2]

Just a few years earlier than *Beloved*'s publication, Davis had written several important essays on slavery. Davis's essays pointed out that books such as Eugene Genovese's *Roll, Jordan, Roll* (1972), Herbert Gutman's *The Black Family in Slavery and Freedom* (1976), and Stanley Elkins's *Slavery* (1959) left out the centrality of Black women and failed to register the impact Black women had on nearly every aspect of slave culture. And thus, Davis insisted on the close analysis of the multidimensional roles of Black women during slavery.[3] Along with Davis, Albert Murray criticized scholars like Elkins for the singularity and vacuity that limited their approach to discussing slaves. Murray claimed that social science fictions and fakelore (a social realism of Black pathology) robbed Black people of the complexity that revealed them as unpredictable and unsettling, not easily circumscribed by racial identity or social environment.[4]

Davis, then, actually found in Morrison's novel what both she and Murray found missing in major slavery studies from the 1950s to the 1980s: "bewildering, outrageous, and terrifying behavior" that was not racially degrading but rather indicative of the enigmatic depths of human social behavior and consciousness.[5] Davis's work pushed for the inclusion, depth of portrayal, persistence, and resistance of slaves, especially Black women; she didn't need *Beloved* to reveal what she already knew in this regard. Thus, what we get from Davis in her awakening through *Beloved* is the strongest implication that it was not just the inclusion or exclusion of Black women's social and political impact that scholars were missing but there was something entirely limiting about how scholars imagined slavery altogether.

Davis's humble and heartfelt insights into Morrison's landmark text lead us to a crucial question. What were the contours, sensibilities, and imaging that shaped Davis's pre-*Beloved* thinking, where slaves' lives appeared singular, one-dimensional, and far less rich with complexity? A crucial part of this chapter is to raise this unidentified backdrop, created through the scholarship of historians like Gutman, Elkins, and perhaps Davis herself, into full view. The aim of this chapter, then, is to demonstrate that there is a *slavery aesthetic* that defines the *imaginative foundation(s)* of slavery scholarship from the 1950s to the 1980s. But the remaining immediate question is: did Morrison's *Beloved* close the book on critical singularity or snug oppositions when it came to discussions of slavery?

According to Stephen Best's claims in *None Like Us* (2018), the answer is absolutely not. Like Davis, Best also sees *Beloved*'s publication as pivotal for critics thinking about slavery; in Best's words, *Beloved* "shaped the way an entire generation of scholars conceived of an ethical relationship to the past."[6] This ethical relation took form in a dialectic between "recovery of the political agency of the enslaved" and acknowledgment that neither scholars nor anyone else can redeem the past.[7] Hence, even though "the *Beloved* moment"[8] largely signaled a renewed fascination with slavery, full of vigorous archival pursuits, the conflict between recovery and melancholic impossibility solidified slavery studies' rigid either/or ethos; slaves remained the pawns in critics' (and politicians') ideological battles over slaves' political consciousness and effectiveness against oppressive institutions.

What I find striking is the unbending through line between Davis's suggestions about the landmark scholarship from the 1950s to 1980s and Best's rendering of scholarship from the 1980s to the present. Both see generations of scholars as offering capacious and interesting contributions to slavery studies yet still withholding the fullness and multidimensionality that Davis witnesses in *Beloved* or the "perverse, queer, and askew" slave subjects Best discovers in Morrison's *A Mercy* (2008).[9] Questions of political agency (or equivalent lexicons[10])—who does or does not have it, how it gets expressed or subjugated, or if one can realize it at all—still hover over slavery scholarship.

With Davis and Best as a point of departure, I submit that *there is* an imaginative field, a slavery aesthetic, that visually, spatially, and rhetorically has impacted what questions we ask and how we analyze slave texts and archives. The best place to begin to prove this claim is Stanley Elkins's influential book *Slavery*, a controversial treatise that energized and exacerbated debates about agency and power in the foundational moment in the study of slavery. In this chapter, I investigate how paradigmatic scholarship on slavery depicted scenes of subjection that are as much visual, spatial, and aesthetic as they are historical. This chapter enriches the ongoing stories from scholars like Davis and Best about what specific modes of thinking shape the current field as well as what we must be prepared to give up in order to see counterlife in slave texts.

Sambo's World

If Helen of Troy's face "launched a thousand ships" and Harriet Beecher Stowe's *Uncle Tom's Cabin* (1852) instigated America's Civil War, then it was Elkins's claim that enslaved Africans were Sambos that ignited a firestorm of controversy and debate among scholars for generations.[11] Elkins published *Slavery: An Intellectual History* in 1959, and in it he claims that the Southern plantation stereotype Sambo was not mere cultural hyperbole but, in fact, the basis of "slave personality."[12] Elkins contends that slavery turned all Africans into obsequious, childlike, and helpless persons who embodied a pure extension of their masters' wishes. Looking back, it almost seems that *Slavery*'s claims were perfectly poised to incense members of the growing Black social movements of the 1960s. These movements swept into the ethos and rationale for the growth of African American studies in universities. Thus, it was not surprising that the response to Elkins from scholars in African American studies was swift and relentless. When looking across decades of slavery studies published after Elkins, one would be hard-pressed to find a seminal work that did not either endorse or dismantle Elkins's infamous Sambo thesis. When Deborah Gray White recounts what inspired but limited her claims from her landmark book *Ar'n't I a Woman* (1985), she focuses on Elkins's field-changing impact.[13] White explains that Elkins inspired a "historiographical movement"—a generation of scholars bent on disproving his claims.[14]

Elkins's Sambo thesis maintained a particular sting because despite the virtues and accomplishments of Black collective political struggles, Elkins insisted that Black radicalism, historical consciousness, and Black culture had little or no effective presence in US slave life. In other words, part of what excited scholars' and activists' interest in recovering slavery is that they looked for hidden gems of social life that evidenced slaves' heroism, agency, and resistance. Almost without exception Elkins downplayed or denied outright this reality of slave culture. Even if scholars interested in slavery did not share Elkins's view that slaves were Sambos, they did share the notion that slavery's brutality heaped irreparable damage on slaves and that white masters indeed had absolute power.

I point to Elkins in particular because his work inspired such passionate responses, but what is equally interesting is that Elkins continued to engage his critics for decades after *Slavery*'s initial publication. His robust engagement gave his work incredible longevity. Elkins insisted on the staying power of his thesis in response to emergent scholarship, and this back-and-forth solidified sides in future debates about the social and political possibilities that slaves created, responded to, or both. Elkins's claims underscore current debates about how to approach slavery in a variety of representations and media. Hence, while more recent scholars have thought that Elkins's Sambo is dead (i.e., thinking about slaves as Sambos), he thrives, cloaked in the conflicts between various rubrics such as damage and resistance, agency and power, and social life and social death.[15]

To depict the antebellum world, Elkins drew on scholarship that was confident in explaining the modern social world. Elkins believed that the slaves' environment was knowable and predictable because it was all part of an identifiable social system. Elkins believed that the plantation was a closed system, no matter how open it may actually appear or one imagines it. I do not use the word *imagine* lightly, and for Elkins to re-create a viable closed system he relied on social scientists' theories of institutional constraint and coercion from the 1940s and 1950s. Perhaps most provocatively, Elkins drew from research on Nazi concentration camps to intensify the sense of being closed in and to make literal the look and effect of social density and the violence of compression. In fact, modernity's institutions, death camps, corporations, and factories were all important to Elkins's understanding of power and violence.

Elkins thought of slaves like characters in a fixed artistic setting where their motivations for acting were completely generated by the environment. His closed system resembled a literal and figurative version of Max Weber's "iron cage."[16] Modern notions of compressed space, whether like Weber's cage or Nazi death camps or images of the Middle Passage, formed Elkins's slavery aesthetic—an imaginative pretext that underscores, crystallizes even, social possibilities in slavery. Elkins's work was crucial in making the vast complexities of slavery and slave social life theoretically digestible— slaves and masters intimately reimagined in miniature cogent boxes. In this way Elkins's slavery concept contains a literary, visual, and spatial sensibility defined by a philosophical supposition; it is possible to produce and maintain a human subject through an elastic web of subjection and damage. What one can also deduce from this supposition is a compelling counterpart: within this endless elastic loop of subjugation is the idea that enslaved Africans take every opportunity to resist and shape meaning in their own lives. These two concepts define slavery studies until this very day.

Through modern social theory, psychoanalytic observations, and Holocaust images, Elkins remade the world of slavery like a snow globe miniature. Slavery scholars still reinforce and reimagine this self-contained world in different ways. The major problem with Sambo's world is that it diminishes the lives of all human subjects involved—slaves, masters, and anyone else. The effect of Elkins's work is that he reduces slaves to either looking for more freedom or succumbing to the impossibility of it. It does not matter if the field of inquiry is closed or open; slavery studies contains an Elkins-inspired pretext, defined by literal and figurative "compression and miniaturization."[17] Thus, Elkins's Sambo thesis, as far as it impacts how we discuss slave texts, is not an easily dismissible set of insults. His sociologically informed slavery aesthetic contains a spatial, social, and philosophical richness that needs to be interrogated and mined for its impact.

This section of the book is a largely diagnostic and descriptive reconceptualization of slavery criticism through Elkins's world of slavery. First, in the following sections I show how Elkins imagined and created slavery as a knowable world where everyone's interest and thinking was reducible to the very environmental structures Elkins chose to identify. Elkins convinced us that having absolute power is not only possible but a worldorganizing social force. He presents this thoroughgoing concept by drawing on modern social theory and historical events to visualize what that power dynamic would look like. With this in mind, I discuss how Elkins's Holocaust depictions helped his readers visualize limited social conditions that made abstract notions of systematic consciousness realizable and concrete. Lastly, I address how versions of Elkins's characters and their antagonists still thrive in the framing and rhetorical schemes of scholars like Saidiya Hartman and Vincent Brown, who emphasize social death or political resistance.

Slavery's Snow Globe

Elkins composes Sambo, his exemplar of slave personality, as an artist would a major character. Sambo is the central figure that animates Elkins's modern literary palette. Elkins's slavery aesthetic permits oversimplifications that still guide the way we approach slavery. Elkins believed that his depiction of Sambo's world would liberate slavery studies, but paradoxically, his impact narrowed it for generations.

In Elkins's eyes, two opposing schools of thought maintained an unbreakable hold on slavery scholarship. These schools were rooted in pro-slavery and abolitionist rhetoric about what was, in fact, the true character of slavery. Elkins wrote a more extensive literature review of influential books and trends in *Slavery*, but he was particularly challenged by the influence of Ulrich Phillips's *American Negro Slavery* (1918) and Kenneth Stampp's refutation of Phillips in *The Peculiar Institution* (1956). Most notably, Phillips agreed with many apologists for slavery, claiming that enslaving Africans was not cruel and unusual; in fact, he claimed, enslaved Africans benefited from the civilizing possibilities of modernizing white society.[18] Stampp's influential book appeared decades after Phillips's and took aim at Phillips's influence over slavery studies. Elkins wrote that Stampp was "locked in struggle with Phillips."[19] Instead of emphasizing slaves' fondness for the benevolent institution, Stampp called attention to slaves' hatred for the system, their courage to resist it, and the variety of expressions of slave life and personality. Elkins attempted to settle the contest between Phillips and Stampp through *Slavery* by arguing that the slaves worked and lived in a closed system that was so brutal it turned them into childlike beings who relied on their masters for all things.

Elkins largely felt successful. Yet, when reflecting on the publication of *Slavery* in the 1970s, he did not realize that settling the "old debate," as he called it, would start another one—which incited far more controversy.[20] When Elkins claimed that the fundamental organizing rubric for understanding slavery was damage, a subsequent generation of scholars argued that enslaved Africans actually resisted their masters whenever possible. Elkins reflected on the damage/resistance debates: "the debate itself, and the rhythm of it, have now taken on qualities uncomfortably similar to those I found so coercive when I first began" contesting the "old debate."[21] Reflecting on his original work, Elkins held greater hopes that his conclusive claims about Sambo would in fact loosen "the coercions of the old debate and open up new lines of exploration."[22] Whether or not Elkins actually ended the debate, he laments that the "new lines" of slavery scholarship he envisioned himself as enabling never actually appeared.

It is clear from Elkins's sparring in *The Debate over Slavery: Stanley Elkins and His Critics* (1971) that slavery scholarship had taken a variety of turns toward Black culture, family life, gender conflict, economics, and the psychology of slavery.[23] Despite the varieties of topics and archives, Elkins found that slavery studies was conceptually stagnant, remaining at square one. Square one means caught in a relentless sense of opposition whose rhetoric remains an extension of, rather than a departure from, the slavery debates that preceded it. Elkins further enshrined, exacerbated even, the sense that scholars' damage claims needed to be proven against scholars' resistance claims again and again. Elkins could not see a way out. "Is there any resolution in sight?" he pondered; he answered: "I have my doubts."[24]

Overlapping senses of irony enveloped Elkins when he first responded to critics of *Slavery*. One irony Elkins was keenly aware of; the other he failed to see. Elkins felt slavery studies had become a closed back-and-forth that he understood better and better through time, but he failed himself to transcend it. Besides this irony a deeper one is worth exploring. It does not dawn on Elkins or his critics that Elkins's constraints from the larger closed argument stem from particular aspects of the closed system itself. The closed system he depicts, his imagined slavery-land, a clear product of modernity, stages the rhetorical and visual space of play for slavery studies' oppositions.

How can rural plantations in the open realms of the American South actually be hermetically sealed? This sense of being closed encourages a limited plane of view rather than an endless horizon of scenarios. In *Slavery*, Elkins drew from the prevailing winds of the social sciences. Scholars became more confident that the real understanding of social reality—the psychology of cultures and practices—was graspable as knowledge produced and understood. In this vein, Henry Adams writes in *The Education of Henry Adams* (1907) that in the period "1793–1893, the American people had hesitated, vacillated, swayed forward and back, between two forces, one simply industrial, the other capitalistic."[25] What is crucial for my interest in Adams is the way he perceives of capitalism in terms of movement in space. He calls it "centralizing, and mechanical."[26] The centralization or centralizing has an image of a locatable epicenter. Adams continues:

> The majority at last declared itself, once and for all, in favor of the capitalistic system with all its necessary machinery. All of one's friends, all of one's best citizens, reformers, churches, colleges, educated classes, had joined the banks to force submission to capitalism; a submission long foreseen by the mere law of the mass. . . . [M]echanical consolidation of force, which ruthlessly stamped out the

life of a class[,] ... created monopolies capable of controlling the new energies that America adored.[27]

Adams writes of control and power of the new energies of capitalism. The spirit of capitalism stamps out life. The opposite of life here is not death specifically. It is the answer to the question of what the opposite is of monopolies, submission, and control. Plurality, defiance, and intractability? Normative life and social trends can now be scientifically identified and tracked as having a powerful governing logic that entrenched people within it—*a system* of power.

Elite families and ruling classes expanded their influence. With added influence in government and industry "men hurried to exploit (and exhaust) the natural and human resources of the country."[28] This social coordination also implied a "systemization of consciousness."[29] People became much more aware of themselves as value, labor processes, and competition and cooperation within advancing technology.[30] Labor conditions, owners, managers, and workers did in fact have to enact systems of labor and new ways of living social life in all its conventions in education, religion, and new communities, which all evolved through the industrial boom of the turn of the century.

This sense of early twentieth-century US history is the backdrop of Elkins's approach to the past and the basis for his thinking about how slavery had an identifiable closed system that one could fully comprehend. Elkins believed Southern plantation slavery was a closed system, but even an open system's centrality and sense of control over normative social, economic, and political conditions already sounded quite closed. Weber describes the modern economic order as "bound to technical and economic conditions of machine production which to-day determine the lives of all the individuals born into this mechanism."[31] Weber crystallized his system and corresponding systemization of consciousness through a striking image: the iron cage.

Like Weber, for Elkins, there is something crucial in imagining and depicting the closed system literally—a construct where concrete bars or walls control the flow of people and ideas in and out. Elkins called slaves "inmates," who internalized their physical constrains with greater intensity than any hegemony could produce on its own. What kind of person emerges from a system like an iron cage, and why do people follow the leadership of corporate, fascist, and political and economic structures? Why is the norm complicity rather than resistance when freedom is so clearly and drastically encumbered? What ideology cements the personality that falls in such self-destructive and delimiting agreement with one's own subjection to state institutions?

To ask these questions in another way: why conceive of antebellum slavery's Sambo in terms of personality? The notion Elkins uses to produce a slave personality comes directly out of the psychologizing of personality after and at the turn of the twentieth century. C. Wright Mills and Hans Gerth studied how the psychic structure of personality maintains a relationship to an individual's social role generally and the opportunities and roles available to that person, as well as enacting a role that incorporates certain values and objectives that steer the person's conduct.[32] Theodor Adorno, Else Frenkel-Brunswik, Daniel Levinson, and Nevitt Sanford's *The Authoritarian Personality* (1950) maintained hope that in studying personality structure in terms of established patterns of "hopes and aspirations, fears and anxieties, that disposed them to certain beliefs and resistant to others," they could establish more precisely why "fascist propaganda fools people."[33] William H. Whyte's *The Organization Man* (1956) worried that the impact of scientism and the waning of the positive attributes of the Protestant ethic made way for the new modern man, who could not only be depicted as man dominated but, worse, as "man surrendering."[34] This modern type resembled an ideal slave; the person of Mills and Gerth and *The Authoritarian Personality* or David Riesman, Nathan Glazer, and Reuel Denney's "lonely crowd" emphasized the challenges of internalized conformity as a result of a cogent and locatable source of power and authority.[35] Elkins did not seek the source of how someone could be unmade but rather sought a "total self" with permanent attributes: a "personality."

Elkins borrowed from social organization theories and came up with something explosive as well as intriguing, stark, and controversial: slaves were Sambos. Elkins agreed that Sambo existed and was not a Southern myth. But who was Sambo really?—a happy-go-lucky socially inferior Black person or the victim of the most heinous violent abuse that created a unique and sustained culture to maintain racial inferiority and social exclusion? Sambo's social reality was undeniable; Elkins contested whether Sambo was a completely white concoction or the result of tireless trauma from an organized system of white supremacy and enslavement. For Elkins could promote and extend the major social sciences back into slavery if he was right about what type of personality slavery produces. Sambo was not in a figurative iron cage but a literal one. But the cage notion came from the open system that contains the centralizing impact of turning a free self into an inmate. Elkins depicts something so extreme and intense that, if believed, uniformly produces imaginable Sambos.[36]

Elkins shared the view of Robert Park and E. Franklin Frazier from the Chicago school of sociology (and later sociologists and anthropologists like Orlando Patterson and Claude Meillassoux) that the trauma and brutality of the Middle Passage as well as strenuous social control of enslavement eviscerated ancestral connections and any West African patterns of culture, connections, and religious expression of being.[37] Elkins maintained no stated interest in such a desire to move across generations like Frazier's *The Negro Family* (1939), but he analyzed more precisely what was true about the inordinate power (normative behavior concerning sex, love, food, and labor) masters had over slaves—to provide a better understanding of how slavery maintained itself and how enslaved Africans internalized precisely what masters wanted them to internalize.

From abolitionist writings, Frazier, Elkins, and others had enough to recount the horror and destructive nature of slavery, but Elkins needed more to construct Sambo with unchangeable personality characteristics, to make Sambo not incidental but a widespread personality characteristic that was more than static and fixed but reproduced itself and endeared itself to the regime that crushed slaves.[38] This was a happy-go-lucky Sambo at heart, a tragedy of trauma that Richard Wright described, like the intensity and compression in Chicago's Black Belt, as a "locked-in life."[39]

Recognizing and succumbing to the absolute power of masters defined Sambo's performative character. Enslaved Africans, despite the appearances of everyday resistance, were fundamentally dependent, childlike, and utterly helpless. Elkins's major evidence of this was that slaves did not organize and risk their lives repeatedly and often to be free. The reason they did not is because the slave master had absolute power. As absolute authorities, the masters define all the terms, and the slaves internalize their masters' desires to the degree that what slaves may perceive as their own interests and desires were really their masters' own. Elkins believed that this totalizing dominance produced Sambo's grave psychological damage—a means of production that endlessly produced its own restraints. An iron cage of culture, ideology, and physical limitation produced, maintained, and reproduced Sambo. From Elkins's perspective, the total self of slave personality was precisely what abolitionists described as a slave having no self. The closed system reoriented slaves to live, desire, laugh, and express other variations of human existence within these confines. Damage, elastic and regenerating, defines Sambo's character; it is the fundamental basis of slavery's mode of production—Elkins's scholarly, yet artistically imagined, sociological vision of the antebellum past.

Mass Appeal

Part of what I want scholars to see about slaves through my counterlife concept is that what masses of enslaved Africans thought and were motivated by is actually unknowable, mysterious at least, and should be pursued with a kind of curiosity that leads to the mishap and confusion of unforeseen significance in slave texts. Elkins and the theorists he both followed and later influenced believed the enslaved Africans were knowable; the compressed violent environment, visual landscape, and the centralizing forces of movement that he constructs as an imaginative gateway into slavery's past were key to this insight. Elkins drew from scholars of modern social control and mass culture such as Walter Benjamin, Theodor Adorno, and Siegfried Kracauer who discussed the way elites, the state, or both control the masses by using figurative language about ideological curtains and iron cages, among other metaphors. This language, imaging, and characterization of a Sambo type constitutes Elkins's own theoretical commitments.

Yet still, Elkins's theoretical version of Sambo's character was insufficient to prove his thesis. He needed something of recent memory, something that weighed heavily on the minds of intellectuals and artists interested in power, conformity, and authority. Elkins drew on the Nazi concentration camps. In his work Elkins openly admits that there are obvious differences between a concentration camp and a Southern plantation. But he insists that the juxtaposition is necessary because the "only *mass experience* Western people have had in recorded history comparable to Negro slavery was undergone in the nether world of Nazism."[40] Elkins felt, above all, that the camps helped him reveal a violent closed system. What makes the concentration camp unique is overt and terrifying brutalization; the control in the concentration camp captures the immediacy of death, an unrivaled exposure to cruelty, and an easily fathomable fixed space.

Elkins's notion of slavery's force depends on the idea of fixed space with little to no outside influence. He does not need the closed system to demonstrate control, but the degree of its closure matters. Small, claustrophobic, degenerate, and unsanitary conditions amplify cruelty and the sense of limitation inside the camp. Elkins likens a human cargo ship from the

FIGURE 1.1 "The Africans of the Slave Bark 'Wildfire'—The slave deck of the
bark 'Wildfire,' brought into Key West on April 30, 1860." Wood engraving.
Source: Library of Congress.

Middle Passage to the railway cars in which Jewish and Polish people, gyp-
sies, and political enemies were transported to Buchenwald.[41]

The ships carrying hundreds of slaves were infamous for conditions
similar to those of the railcars used by the Nazis. Space is crucial for shock
and disorienting detachment and does not stop with ships or railcars. Even
when Nazi victims arrived they were housed in barracks, piled one on top
of the other. Elkins does not describe these conditions in the book, but
since 1945 the availability of photos and film documenting the concentration camps had increased. Although the reality of the Nazi extermination

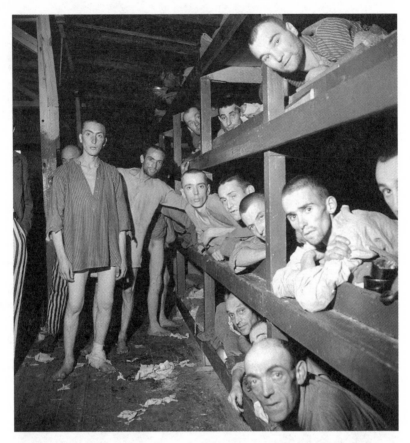

FIGURE 1.2 *Buchenwald*, Margaret Bourke-White, 1945. Time and Life Pictures. Courtesy of *Life* magazine.

of Jewish people did not grab firm footing in the American consciousness until the 1970s, in 1945 *Life* magazine published photos of Buchenwald that showed massive overcrowding, structures of containment, enclosures where people labored to death, gas chambers, stacked prisoners, two-to-four-storied enclosures of cement, and large warehouses.[42]

Such physical limitation has an immense effect on social relations and circumstances. The closed system's image and actual limited space suggest overwhelming intensity, like in other modern spaces from Chicago's Black Belt or of poor people piled on top of one another, as in the late-1800s photographs of Jacob Riis. Elkins wants to produce "Sambo" as a primary way of demonstrating the guards' inhumane treatment of the prisoners, how dependent the inmates were on the guards, and the lack of revolts or sustained resistance.

The images, whether revealed by Elkins or in *Life*, alone present the viewer with questions. What could the person or people do to escape or alleviate this condition? What are the cultural inputs and relations concerning such conditions? According to Elkins, the only input is the Nazis, who built the concentration camp, but Elkins's questions stem from his belief in the social reality of the Nazis' absolute power. Thus, the camp presents nothing but circumscribed space, where the architects of the camp achieve their desired results. Elkins insisted, "Expectation and performance coincide exactly."[43] The visualized cramped space places people in situations where there are no options, only thoughts of the lack of options that define all the conditions of possibility. Then once one introduces the imminent and impending violence, it all makes perfect sense as a self-contained, hermetically sealed space, where violence, pain, and consequences reproduce themselves in a variety of ways that produce a single type of person, a slave personality, Sambo.

Elkins said there were exceptions to Sambo's slave personality like craftsmen, mechanics, barbers, and preachers, but they became leaders outside of or on the outskirts of "the full coercions of the plantation authority system."[44] They boarded trade vessels or were part of bustling urban centers. These images of the openness of the sea, circuits of travel and trade, or international exchange instead of the overloaded images of a closed system provided a dynamic and variant environment. The alternative urban center or sea traffic present a different set of questions about what manumitted slaves or persons would do and who they would talk to in "free states or Canada."[45] Limitations are left abstract by Elkins. The entire social system that Elkins conceives of is wide open and only helps Elkins reinforce the dramatic constraint of his closed system, Sambo, and what kind of environment it would take to not be a Sambo. According to Elkins's line of thought, if you believe slavery was intense and brutal social control and not like a "free state or Canada," then you're stuck with his Sambo slave type. The modern photograph, aided by industry, technology, modernity itself, helps to reinforce Elkins's claims about Sambo's world. From Elkins's viewpoint, which some theorists still maintain, whatever slaves do within that regime can be read as an extension of the regime itself.

But this version of Elkins's slavery aesthetic, Sambo's world making, is world crushing because the sense of structure, both real and imagined, as Weber's iron cage and/or Elkins's literal cage, dwarfs and subsumes collective and individual social concerns that cannot be predicted or foreseen by the goals of reproducing the system. One recalls Louis Althusser's opening in his famous essay on ideology: "The ultimate condition of production is therefore the reproduction of the condition of production." This system prevents participants of "everyday consciousness" from raising themselves "to the point of view of production."[46] If what we believe or know is the condition of production, produced abstractly as slavery, slavery's regime, white supremacy, or all three, then acts for or against the system can be reduced to it.

Whether Sambo exists is a question that relies on a point of view about structure, power, and their effects on groups and individuals. Sambo's type evinces a visual, spatial, and behavioral plane of mass experience, and in this mass experience the imagined individual dies unless he exists solely to be comprehended as a feature of mass experience. In Elkins's slavery aesthetic we can only imagine that most people never gain the "point of view of production," and it is our job to attempt to retrieve from the archive that, even if they did gain that ground of insight, because the system was not overthrown, enslaved Africans were effectively subdued by it. But is this where we should stop when it comes to representations of enslaved Africans and what slaves produced? Are we still locked in a bizarre mirror of Elkins's line of thinking and assumptions?

Walking Dead

Elkins's slavery aesthetic thrives in the veins of current slavery studies. Elkins contends that the entire social life of the slave was under the thumb of the master, not just in written law or by physical punitive demand, but that overall, in mind, body, and soul the slaves were possessed by masters. Orlando Patterson said that slave reality is no social life at all and called the fundamental condition of the slave "social death." Elkins's slavery aesthetic forms the backdrop that helps us make sense of the claim that a variegated and vibrant social milieu can be best described as its opposite, social death. Unlike Elkins's largely forgotten slave personality, there are no shortages of reference to Patterson's arresting phrase, *social death*. With referential ease, scholars draw on Patterson to point to the relentless violence slaves experienced, slaves' estrangement from their native cultures and ancestors, and the near impossibility of slaves' pursuit of meaning in their lives for themselves. Borrowing from Patterson, critics also use the term *social death* (or its cousin, *civic death*) to depict conditions in prisons, immigration conflicts, or any other social conditions that warrant the startling and bleak impression of the term.[47] There should be no doubt that social death—articulated as social realism, mere metaphor, or theoretical point of view—has shaped slavery studies and studies of other tragic and unjust social conditions.

What I put forth here is while the offensive Sambo does not appear in Patterson's masterwork as a key player or in those critics inspired by Patterson's work, the crucial elements that make Sambo possible are made manifest in social death as well as in other ur-texts like Hartman's *Scenes of Subjection*. Thus, in Hartman's *Scenes* or Patterson's *Slavery and Social Death* or in waves of scholarship both influenced and inspired by them lie the invisible but flourishing vines of Elkins's slavery aesthetics and its masterful encoding of absolute power and manifold violence that cannot be redressed. What unites Elkins, Patterson, and Hartman is the expressed and implied concept of *absolute power* (total domination, total abjection, or other "totals")—a term that, while present and significant in the work of each of these scholars, is still expressed differently by each—reiterating elasticity and the near-impregnable nature of slavery's regime (the idea of a closed, unified, and coherent regime). Vincent Brown contended that one of the definitive features of social death was disconnection from ancestors and cultural traditions (anticipated by sociologists Robert Park, E. Franklin Frazier, and Elkins), but Brown misses that absolute power is the staple feature of Patterson's that coheres a system that can produce and maintain social death everywhere in all slaves.[48]

Patterson's claims about social death, unlike Elkins's claims about slave culture, do not rely on revealing an actual closed system. Slavery, as Patterson defined it, "was the permanent, violent domination of natally alienated and generally dishonored persons" and did not need to be illustrated by concepts of literal walls like Elkins referenced through relying on the Holocaust.[49] For Patterson, the brutal treatment of slaves, their desire to belong to or be incorporated in a family or clan after being uprooted from it, and the pursuit to honor or redeem their status as slaves all served the slave masters' interest. This social umbrella, defined and controlled solely on the masters' terms, sustained masters' absolute power. Without a literal closed system, Patterson produced a sense of a tightly knit logic like Weber's iron cage. It makes sense in terms of space, limits, and field of view; yet there is no actual field beyond the cultures and ideology of slavery's regime. The strangling logic is like the widespread dissemination of deadly gas, physically nowhere yet everywhere—its presence is felt wherever power can be reinforced.

Patterson's exception to absolute power returns us to something akin to Elkins's thinking about a closed system. If the slaves themselves practiced a "truly vibrant slave culture, if it is to avoid the crisis of honor and recognition, [then they] must have a substantial free population."[50] To repeat, Elkins believed in exceptions to Sambo's obsequiousness and helplessness in areas where there are more free Blacks—where possibilities exist for more cross-cultural pollination: dynamic and open areas rather than closed. Patterson also imagines most slave societies, if not physically homogeneous, were able to keep slaves away from the "substantial free population" so that slaves continued to seek recognition, honor, and full incorporation in society. In Patterson's view, slaves weren't infantile, docile, deceptive jokesters as Elkins claimed, but they wanted recognition and honor from their masters' culture. While Patterson did not see a "truly vibrant slave culture" like other scholars during this era, slaves' honor means that slaves contained an existentially human component, an innate sense of dignity. Tragically their masters used this sensibility to manipulate them through violence and other forms of coercion.

The ideological and disciplining practices function with such effect that what Elkins sought to demonstrate in a closed system Patterson captures without one. But Patterson's emphasis on slaves' isolation from free populations reinforces a sense that slave populations could be absolutely controlled, which is a closed system in effect. The other key dimension of Patterson that mirrors Elkins is that slavery was elastic and "was a self-correcting institution: what it denied the slave it utilized as the major means of motivating him."[51] This airtight logic of practice demonstrated a condition that was intense, claustrophobic, and violent. Even the prospect of manumission was used to ensure the reinforcement of slavery's constraints. The absolute power in Elkins and Patterson ensured the violence-induced motivation of "slavery, as an enduring social process."[52]

Patterson maintains the sense that an airtight system could be open or closed but nonetheless had a fail-safe grip on all slaves. But slavery scholars don't see how slave life becomes knowable and predictable just by knowing that the person's social position is that of a slave. Patterson did not make this claim about the precise thoughts of slaves' and masters' interiority, but he did everything to imply a structure where the individual thoughts of actors in slavery was nearly irrelevant and inconsequential because of the seismic impact of the imposing structure of the slaveholding regime.

There is no greater example of the school of absolute power that Elkins popularized and Patterson amplified than Hartman's book *Scenes of Sub-*

jection. What I am looking for with *Scenes* as with *Social Death* is how the story of absolute power and the impact of a closed system like Elkins's captures and intimates, visualizes and projects changes in lexicon and archive but remains remarkably consistent in its voice and in the scholarly conversations it inspires.[53] Hartman's version of absolute power is the most provocative because she doesn't rely on a closed system like Elkins or slaves' proximity to freed persons like Patterson; her concept of subjection relies on the overarching violence, ideology, and circuits of power not only in slavery but in emancipated life. With dramatic intensity, Hartman's analysis exposes the desolate fragility of Black freedom.

Hartman has the most dynamic and expanded sense of being closed in by the tentacles of white supremacy. For Hartman every utterance of humanity, self, and autonomy not only is corrupted by the subjection of enslaved Africans but is constituted by it. Hartman expands the concept behind slavery and social death, which is largely one regime, one system, that entangles and reinforces itself most urgently in the places one denies its presence. So we know the violent subjugation of the auction block, but innocent amusements of Black culture bear the mark of white supremacy and tactical oppression. For Hartman, this is where the "stranglehold of slavery" is the most sinister and lethal.[54]

Sambo appears in Hartman with surprising likeness to Elkins's rendition, though reinvented and updated. For Hartman, "Sambo conjures up an idealized and fetishized state of servitude," and his voice hides slaves' horrors and simulation of will, the pleasure of singing for master, and effectively "annuls any possibility of redress or resistance."[55] This concept is what Hartman turns to again and again, leaving no stone unturned, no aspect of slave life untouched by slavery's "endless litany of violence."[56] This turns what I would call a complicated and diverse terrain of culture into a small field of ideology and action. Slavery is immortal and self-correcting even decades after Lincoln signed the Emancipation Proclamation. Like Elkins's sync between structure and slave or Patterson's self-correcting system, Hartman sees slavery's power to reproduce itself everywhere as a governing logic.

Patterson's references to Frederick Douglass or his anecdotes from field anthropology only gesture to slave interiority. Hartman moves deeper into slaves' interiority. Hartman's interests in literature, letters, and personal stories give one the impression of how slavery maintains a stranglehold on interior life. There is no place slavery's violence does not infiltrate, destroy, and seek its own end or hide itself in the moment it is stealing the subjectivity a slave subject seems perfectly poised to claim. But there is an interesting question of degree here. Hartman's work was powerful, new, and frightening because of the degree of entanglement and the inescapability produced by her vision of slavery. This claustrophobic entanglement, this web, is another version of a closed system because the open and free subjectivity perishes on utterance. This is a version of the absolute power of a closed system, a thoroughgoing violence that maintains elasticity to snuff out or repurpose anything that looks like resistance, redress, or agency. This is the "stranglehold of slavery" in Hartman's words.

Absolute power, Sambo's slave personality, social death, or scenes of subjection turn slavery into slavery aesthetics' snow globe. With the help of modern urban experiences of compression, photography, and social theory, Elkins created this imaginative looking glass. The terrain of action and play within a closed system or an open system with an airtight logic makes all points of stimuli from various human behaviors and thoughts reducible to the discernable structure that we clearly imagine. But the gift of imaginative clarity of this mode of thinking is its biggest problem. Social reality's many dimensions and conflicts and expressions are often foggy, elusive, enigmatic, and challenging for discerning the origins of motivations and realizations. Thus, while these titans of "absolute power" differ about how masters made total domination manifest, they fundamentally agree on the cogent, clear field or system, where the motivations of the actors and agents to resist or succumb are always clear.

Woke Work

As I mentioned earlier, Deborah Gray White identifies Elkins as a particular catalyst that dominated critical attention. White, on the scope of her own work, claimed that she and other scholars of Black life founded a "historiographical movement" bent on proving Elkins wrong, and this meant finding more avenues of Black resistance, especially for enslaved Black women.[57] Elkins, Patterson, and Hartman tend to encourage critical responses. David Scott depicted such responses: as scholars of slavery and colonialism we are asked "to look for agency that transgresses" masters' power, strictures of white supremacy, or both.[58] I am not interested merely in showing how scholars detailed various evidence of Black resistance. Working through seminal claims about Black resistance helps me demonstrate the difficulty of outstripping the initial field Elkins established. In scholarly disagreement with absolute power, social death, and total domination, did scholars of resistance and agency further cement the slavery aesthetic of a closed system, a series of monolithic dialectics that still reign today?

Ralph Ellison, for example, repeatedly and often warned against using categories and theories to fully depict Black life, especially because sociologists and historians, like Frazier, Park, Gunnar Myrdal, and Elkins, failed to present anything about Black social life that was not the result of white domination. If Elkins, Patterson, and Hartman were right, then domination is not one of the factors when discussing slavery and its aftermath but *the* factor. When Elkins looked for a conceptual source to locate the origins of Black cultural resistance in scholarship he found it in Ellison's essays. Elkins credits Ellison with influencing a generation of scholars "absorbed with resistance and culture."[59] How much Ellison actually had to do with the flurry of scholarship that emphasized resistance, agency, and Black culture is debatable. What is fair to say is that Myrdal's *American Dilemma* (1944) and Daniel Patrick Moynihan's *Report on the Negro Family* (1965) provoked Ellison's intellectual and political hostilities. Ellison repeated, as often as he could, that Black people and culture were defined by transformative and heroic actions. US Black people made a way of life, Ellison emphasized; one could not understand that way of life during and after slavery by starting and ending with the indefatigable hold of white domination.

Ellison argued that studies of Black experience, which relied on the explanatory power of sociology and social theory, often missed the "great deal of heroism" in Blacks' struggles.[60] He insisted that slaves played a crucial role in American culture, and slave being was both a product of "brutalization" and "that culture"; the "culture" Blacks produced falls by the wayside in Elkins's slavery.[61] Thus Ellison, while not advocating for an African survivalist or a Black revolutionary ethos, pushed the idea that Blacks were cocreators of an expressive culture that allowed them to survive and endure in conditions where whites in power physically brutalized, politically excluded, and socially demonized them. Ellison established an implicit connection between the rhetoric of heroism and Black social production in everyday life. But must heroism or political possibility be implied or stated explicitly to make slaves' lives worthy of study? How does this expectation shape what types of slave actions, meaning making, and survival tactics are the focus of scholarly attention?

More important, Elkins claimed that his disagreement with Ellison encouraged a generation of counter-Sambo (counter-Elkins, rather) texts—books on slavery that featured resistance and Black culture. Blassingame's *The Slave Community* (1979), Peter Wood's *Black Majority* (1966), and Herbert Gutman's *The Black Family in Slavery and Freedom* (1976) all had a lasting impact on American slavery studies. Eugene Genovese's *Roll, Jordan, Roll: The World the Slaves Made* (1972), however, stands out as garnering the most attention. Genovese demonstrated with painstaking detail his subtitle: the chattel South was a "world" that "the slaves made." Genovese depicted slaves as makers and producers of music, culture, architecture, and religious rituals that shaped slaves' understanding of and negotiation with the slaveholders' regime. Like Ellison, Genovese suggested that Black culture making under slavery was heroic. Yet despite Genovese's tremendous respect for slave culture, he laments that, whatever slaves' heroics, the slaves ultimately acquiesced. Genovese crystallized the challenge across the board between resistance and damage: did slave culture actually threaten slave masters, or did it ultimately make them better adapted to their lives as slaves and "reinforce the regime"?[62] While he offers a great deal more evidence, including broadening the archives, than Elkins, Genovese seems very interested in questions similar to those of Elkins. Thus, while Genovese saw his work as refuting Elkins's and expanding the study of slavery, *Roll, Jordan, Roll* made concrete the poles of disagreement about the relationship between slave resistance and masters' power.

Patterson reviewed Genovese's tour de force in the *New Republic*, in which he focused on Genovese's failure to answer one pressing question: why weren't slaves more heroic? Patterson wanted to know the "reasons for slaves' acquiescence."[63] While "expressive components" of slave culture were impressive in music, Patterson concluded, slaves' resistance efforts were inconsequential, a "total betrayal of . . . the *heroic ideals* of their African ancestors."[64]

My point is not to come down on the side of either heroes or Sambos, agents or those that knowingly or unknowingly acquiesced, but to reveal the staying power of this binary that has such a tight grip on slavery studies. Even recently Patterson's *Slavery and Social Death* was taken up for its ongoing influence in slavery scholarship. Vincent Brown has taken up the oppositions discussed in this essay to unsettle the growing scholarly commitment to Patterson's social death. After the publication of his book on the funeral rituals of Jamaican slaves, *The Reaper's Garden* (2008), Brown embraced the challenge of evaluating the work of scholars who deployed social death as a prism. In "Social Death and Political Life in the Study of Slavery," Brown juxtaposes his own approach to slavery in Jamaica with works like Stephanie Smallwood's *Saltwater Slavery* (2007), Ian Baucom's *Specters of the Atlantic* (2005), and Hartman's *Scenes* (1997) and *Lose Your Mother* (2007).

Brown's crucial conclusion in the essay, however, is his assertion that studying slavery sheds light on how "conflicts over the most elemental aspects of social life informed" major events of political history.[65] The question I ask of Brown is, why the endgame of "political history"? While Brown points us to the import of common acts that other scholars overlook, he still reinforces the relevance of slave choices and actions to influence politics and political history. The subtext of Brown's emphasis is that slaves' choices, practices, and culture, even ones that have eluded scholars, can be significant to the larger events scholars already deem monumental. Brown suggests that, while slave actions may not be heroic, their importance is of heroic proportion and of consequence to politics and political thinking.

Can slave culture, thought, and practices capture values and significance outside of agential politics, or is there only a political history of slave social life? Brown demonstrates in *The Reaper's Garden* that one can deemphasize the language of agency and resistance and emphasize "social being," but is this really still just a subtle way of demonstrating slaves' impact on their masters and their world-making culture without explicitly drawing on the contested phrases of past slavery debates? Brown still seems trapped in the very oppositions he wants to escape. He advances his profound thesis on "political life" against other slavery arguments that rely too heavily on social death, damage, and idioms of absolute power.

Stock Figures

Sambo's stock figure, a cultural abstraction, which Elkins rendered historically and psychologically through his slavery aesthetic, revealed the damaged and compressed existence of enslaved Africans. For Elkins slave personality was only possible in a closed system, but Patterson's "social death" and Hartman's subjection showed that even if the system wasn't literally closed like a concentration camp, the violent force of white domination functioned spatially and imaginatively like Weber's iron cage metaphor. Elkins and others worried that simply reversing Sambo for heroes and agents or metaphors like social death to social/political life would turn slavery studies into a field framed by snug and static historical opposites. But Elkins's warning (which he failed to heed himself) can also be read as an indictment of the potential oversimplification of slavery's social reality.

Can we have it both ways? Can we frame discussions of slave life and culture in oppositional dyads like social death/social life or brutalization/resistance and still keep in view the radical refusals and unsettling ambivalence of enslaved Africans? This defines so much of slavery studies scholarship, but there is a problem in fully being attentive to both fluidity and definitional categories. What slavery studies has shown before and after *Beloved* is that scholarship can have complexity and address ambiguity but still reproduce slavery aesthetics' cage, the sense of the closed system, the claustrophobic back-and-forth.

When the late Ira Berlin warned that slavery studies is too full of "stock figures of the scholarly imagination," either he's wrong, or we can have diversity of archive and practice yet still produce firm frames and binding oppositions no matter the period and geography.[66] I think Berlin (as well as Ellison and a few other artists) pointed us in the right direction that scholars have yet to fully take seriously in their approach to slavery and slaves' representations. Berlin wrote, "Knowing that a person is a slave doesn't tell you everything about him or her," and "understanding that a person was a slave was not the end of the story but the beginning."[67]

I am trying to show in this chapter that escaping the cloaked grip of Elkins's slavery aesthetic and its aftermath is much harder than we imagine. Herman Melville's 1855 novella "Benito Cereno" contains an answer to shrugging off Sambo's cloak. Melville shows his readers the significance of not knowing and realizing one's ignorance when it comes to what a slave is thinking or why they may do what they do. In "Benito Cereno," two Spanish friends Aranda and Benito Cereno are transporting slaves along with other cargo in the Americas. One part of the novella scholars pay little attention to is that it is Benito Cereno's dear friend Aranda who assures him that he knows his slaves and that they are safe to sleep on deck without their chains. It is clear that he has every reason to believe that Babo, Atufal, and the other enslaved Africans will not disrupt the voyage and be obedient. He knows their history and psychology. He knows the slaves' interiors well. But, in a bloody mockery of Aranda's certainty, the enslaved Africans revolt. They kill Aranda and demand their freedom.

My point about the novella has nothing to do with slave resistance or how the slaves performed their objecthood throughout the text or what made them somehow complicit with their own subjection. What we can take from the story is what made Aranda so certain about his slaves? What were the social cues and constraints around their thinking and responses? How could he be so confident in their obedience that he would risk his own life on it? Aranda and Benito Cereno are not just wrong about what is inside the revolting Africans' heads; they're wrong about what people can do, what conditions affect them at different times, and that overall social relations are multifaceted and unpredictable. If we take the latter series of possibilities more seriously, it is hard to tarry in what Berlin called slavery studies' "stock figures of the scholarly imagination."[68] To fully embrace Berlin's foresight, in the remainder of this book, I assume that as we get closer to slaves as individuals or within a community they'll likely exceed any frame or system we can contain them in.[69] With this concept in mind, we can discover, confront, examine, and relay the *counterlife* of enslaved Africans.

2

KALEIDOSCOPE VIEWS

Once I took white people out, it's like the whole world
opened up; you can imagine anything, everything.
—Toni Morrison, *Proceed with Caution*, BBC documentary, 2015

I spent the introduction and first chapter of this book explaining how the core of slavery studies still wears Sambo's cloak. Sambo's cloak, as I put it in the last chapter, is defined by Stanley Elkins's slavery aesthetic, which compresses and diminishes how we can imagine the range of motivations behind what slaves thought and practiced. The effect of this diminishing of the social field is that scholars too often wed slavery's significance to its measurable political impacts. Discovering counterlife in slavery's archives and texts means wrestling with Sambo's cloak in order to traverse it. With this insight, I focus on slave texts with a keen eye toward slavery's significance—not resting easy in any particular political valence but instead revealing simultaneous points of view. I think about this simultaneous view as a kaleidoscope lens through which different faces of counterlife appear.

This chapter examines seminal works by Frederick Douglass, Radcliffe Bailey, and Edward Jones. What is most interesting about their portrayals of slavery is how they stabilize personal identity, what it means to be historical, and sociological certainty, only to thoroughly stretch and deform these concepts at the same time. Bailey's installations, Douglass's descriptions of Sandy's root from the *Narrative of the Life*, and Alice's "creation" from Jones's *Known World* supply fertile ground on which to render counterlife. Douglass, Jones, and Bailey present revelations of truth in these works, but then, just as quickly as reliable truths are powerfully revealed, these hard facts become troubling, enigmatic, even incoherent. These texts strongly suggest that unraveling truth at the moment a subject achieves clarity about it is also a crucial and undeniable fact of social reality that critics do not take seriously enough, especially when approaching slave texts.

In Douglass's *Narrative* (1845) his friend Sandy gives him a root in the middle of a chapter where Douglass arguably solidifies his identity in manhood, Christianity, and freedom. But the root's role in this chapter is mystical because it troubles some of the very facts about Douglass's religious beliefs, bravado, and moral certainty, which Douglass appears to show with unambiguous clarity. Bailey's installations also draw on undeniable constellations of facts—biographical facts, historical and political events. Bailey elevates history only to blur it and recast it in methods, textures, and other unexpected expressions. Bailey toys, torments, and reveals slavery's presence like a trickster. His works on the Middle Passage in *Memory as Medicine* (2011) establish solid ground with history, materials, and themes and then unsettle these relations repeatedly, undermining any concrete victory for facing history's past or a usable realization that slavery is, in fact, still with us. Just as Bailey brings his viewers in to the realm of the trickster, Alice from Jones's *The Known World* (2004) epitomizes it. Alice is assumed to be mentally ill, socially misguided, and a nuisance. Jones transforms her character into the most profound leader and creator of meaning in the book. Alice Night's creations defy all genres of art and categories of experience. Jones's novel and characters invite the reader into a positivistic material account of slavery, a kind of faux social realism, and then most effectively through Alice, Jones frustrates the readers' expectations of what is true and can be known.

I emphasize throughout this chapter that the critic must accept as well as inhabit multiple and competing layers and voices in the text. James Baldwin captures this idea when he describes how history gets expressed in spirituals: "History becomes a garment that we can wear, and share, and not a cloak in which to hide, and time becomes a friend."[1] The process of wearing history, putting it on and taking it off as an individual, is like sharing and reading or experiencing the manifold depth of an art installation. Slave texts' aesthetics of history, the realization of history's uncanny expression becoming present through art, is not one that lends itself to instrumentality through politicized awakenings, inspiring targeted actions, or the precise action of consciousness. What is mesmerizing and profound is that slavery's art can be most forceful not in spite of its arresting simultaneity but because of it; these are slavery's lasting impressions that we may not expect—profound, yet outstripping any immediately usable truths.

Roots

If any person rests on sure footing as a symbol for slaves' quest for freedom it is Douglass.[2] Douglass's autobiographical writing contains a surprising set of discrepancies that can shed further light on what I mean by counterlife. Douglass's writings cast the hero as decisively manly, undoubtedly Christian, and exceedingly rational. These are all enlightened, stable values of Western culture, how one practices ideal citizenship and membership in a modern democratic community. But Douglass's writings, which anchor the pillars of modern civilization's striving, carry the underside of darkness, unsanctioned play, and untoward behaviors and motivations that defy the stability Douglass projects. In perhaps the most definitive moment, Douglass indulges in the devil's root work to get himself out from under the thumb and whip of the dastardly Edward Covey.

Covey is the overseer; he breaks slaves and thus symbolizes the widespread cruelty of slavery's dehumanizing process. When Douglass, with a root and his fist, defeats Covey, he says he will continue to be a slave in form but not in fact. What type of self and corresponding social relations with others permits Douglass to be a slave in form but not a slave in fact? The straightforward reading is Douglass will imitate a content slave; he will be a convincing version of content slave while, in reality, being utterly discontent. When Douglass proclaims he will be a slave only in form, he does not mention the root Sandy gives him; but, I submit, the root constitutes the slave form/fact performance. In this section, I'm interested in the connection between Douglass as he presents the root and how the root signals profound destabilization, where Douglas appears the most certain about his identity and future. It is important to analyze how the root, and

Douglass's relationship with Sandy, defines Douglass's identity by unsettling the picture of Douglass's religious beliefs, interpersonal connections, and moral convictions.

With the root by his side, Douglass overtakes his overseer Covey. After Douglass pummels Covey, he reflects on his awakening in spiritual terms: "It was a glorious resurrection": Douglass journeyed "from the tome of slavery to the heaven of freedom."[3] How is Douglass, an icon of the good, of intelligence, of masculine courage, and divine fortune, also defined by the devilish magical power of "black art"?[4] In *Narrative* (1845), he validates the root, and in *My Bondage, My Freedom* (1855), he disowns it. I see this discrepancy about the root as an opportunity to think about Douglass through counterlife—to view him as contradictory and irreducible in a moment that contains a strong emphasis on solidifying Douglass's identity, masculinity, and political prowess. The root moment simultaneously conveys a self-problematic in Douglass that troubles established renderings of a singular subject with a coherent set of values, commitments, and everyday life practices. I demonstrate that the root turns Douglass into Douglasses, a sense of multiplicity where Douglass maintains a singular focus and yet produces enigmas that reveal their own kind of importance as ongoing destabilizers of social relations between himself and others like his dear friend Sandy.

Narrative, My Bondage, and *Life and Times* (1893) all contain Douglass's pivotal fight with Covey the Negro breaker. Douglass's unexpected defeat of Covey unites each version. Before the fight Douglass explains that his friend Sandy gives him a root and insists that no white man will able to whip him. After his victory over Covey, Douglass confirms Sandy's proclamation, writing: "from this time . . . I was never fairly whipped."[5] When it comes to Sandy's root work, "The Last Flogging" in *Life and Times* and *My Bondage* are nearly identical, but the difference between Douglass's *Narrative* and the subsequent writings is quite striking. In 1845's *Narrative*, Douglass stages the root, its potential power, and its value as a central question, and in 1855 the root is almost incidental, merely a way to introduce his good friend Sandy. The difference in the texts provides an opportunity to revisit the root's value, Sandy's significance, and Douglass's relationship to both. The interplay I read in the two texts disturbs what meaning Douglass finds in the root and the moral and social value medicinal healers have to Douglass and other members of the slave community.

The first time Douglass introduces us to Sandy, Douglass has hidden himself in the woods after Covey beat him. He was covered in blood and desperate and had no place to go. Fortunately, Douglass "fell in with Sandy Jenkins," a slave with whom he was somewhat acquainted.[6] Douglass knew enough about Sandy to know that Sandy had a wife and that Sandy was on his way to visit her. Without explanation, Douglass confides in Sandy, who comes across as a patient and concerned listener. He listens to the "whole matter over," explains Douglass.[7] Worried about Douglass's condition and his future, the "old adviser" offers a natural supernatural proposal. Sandy changes quickly from mere acquaintance to confidant and adviser. Sandy insists that Douglass find a certain root and carry it on his right side, in order to prevent any white man from whipping him. After initially rejecting the idea, Douglass takes the root to please Sandy and then returns to Covey. Douglass notices a change in Covey's demeanor immediately and does not know whether to give credit to the root or to the Sabbath day. Douglass leaves it an open question but subsequently declares that it was on Monday morning when the "virtue of the root was fully tested."[8] The reader sees no more about Sandy in the immediate moments, but Douglass cannot be whipped as Sandy professed; he defeats Covey. Douglass's triumph indicates that he's battle tested for freedom and the root played a role in the raising of Douglass's "long-crushed spirit."[9] Douglass leaves every impression that Sandy's wisdom pays off in his first *Narrative*. Still, ambiguity lingers because Douglass does not come right out and say it, and this lingering ambiguity is also important—it's Douglass's partiality, his partial purchase, that leaves the residue of uncertainty.

My Bondage's root episode is decisively different. Douglass filled it with new and different information and emphases. In *Narrative*, Douglass confirms the root's power. In *My Bondage*, however, Douglass rejects the root and its validity altogether; root talk, Douglass writes, was "absurd, ridiculous, if not positively sinful."[10] He attributes all of Sandy's help not to the "black art" but to being exhausted without resources and to his being discovered by a caring "good Samaritan."[11] He does not just fall in with Sandy. Sandy discovers him bloody and beaten in the woods. In *My Bondage*, Sandy is clearly famous for his "good nature" and "good sense."[12] Sandy has a kind, religious wife who values spending the holy day as free time with her husband. It is only by knowing that "the Lord" was somehow involved that encourages Douglass to take the root from Sandy.

When Douglass returns to Covey in the 1855 rendering, it is no longer in question whether Covey's demeanor change could be attributed to the root or to the Sabbath. The Sabbath, not the root, was "the real explanation" for Covey's dramatic change in manner.[13] The biggest change, however, is that Douglass does not mention the root's virtue being tested through the outcome of the fight as he does in the *Narrative*. But what he does make clear is that when he confronts Covey the root is gone from his mind completely. "I now forgot my roots." He demands that the reader attribute the action to his own "pledge to stand up in my own defense."[14] Douglass affirms himself; he credits his own individual will. Douglass eliminates all doubt in *My Bondage*; it was not Sandy's root but instead the Lord's favor and Douglass's determined resistance. But by going through this major reversal, does Douglass undermine his own efforts to minimize the root and, instead, actually magnify the root's import?

The effect of minimizing the root in 1855 makes its emphasis in 1845 more interesting—even compelling. The certainty of *My Bondage* is most profound because of the uncertainty located in the *Narrative*. Clarity in *My Bondage* confirms the utter ambiguity of the *Narrative*. So what does Douglass believe, or rather, what is the culture of belief and practice that makes the tension between these texts significant? Will the real Douglass please stand up, or perhaps it is the notion of a real Douglass that is the fiction created by the discrepancies between the two texts? What if Douglass was not wandering at all while he was desperate and wounded but looking for Sandy precisely because he had no other options? Douglass, a sociologist and an embodiment of slave life, is well aware of the "magical powers" that stem from Sandy's background as a "genuine African."[15] Perhaps Douglass found root work and rituals appealing like other enslaved Africans. Douglass provides no conclusive answers and leaves these questions open.

Giving Sandy's character greater context can tell us more about Douglass's fortunate run-in with him. W. E. B. Du Bois depicts someone in *The Souls of Black Folk* (1903) who resembles Douglass's Sandy. Du Bois explains, the "medicine-man . . . appeared on the plantation and found his function as the healer of the sick, the interpreter of the Unknown, the comforter of sorrowing, the supernatural avenger of wrong, and the one who rudely but picturesquely expressed the longing, disappointment, and resentment of a stolen and oppressed people."[16] This list of attributes sounds like a neat summary, but if one imagines a situation with numerous slaves, what Du Bois depicts covers an infinite variety of possibilities, frustrations, and experiences—just about everything. Sandy is a healer and a counselor full of wisdom, and in this role he would need to be capable of meeting the emotional, spiritual, and physical needs of slaves—relations between slaves and masters, slaves and other laborers, slaves and slaves, and individual slaves within themselves. If healers are around, who else does one turn to in moments of desperation, where one is bloodied in body and depressed in spirit, but to one who is wise, comforting, and gifted with advice for remedying ailments.[17] Henry Bibb and William Wells Brown both sought out medicine men for different reasons—for love, physical healing, spiritual blessings, the prevention of masters' abuses. Slave masters knew of people like Sandy. They were feared, loathed, and tolerated. Albert Raboteau claims that conjuring, ghost-lore, witchcraft, and herbalism constituted a rich tradition in slave quarters.[18]

Discussing the 1845 *Narrative*, sociologist Paul Gilroy sees Sandy as an authority figure, as a practitioner of conjuring, an "Africentric" alternative.[19] For Gilroy, Douglass's root moment contains a "deployed ambiguity," a series of binaries that Douglass invites the reader to entertain: two clear alternatives in Douglass.[20] Gilroy does not explicitly state the alternatives, but they appear from his use of the term *Africentric*: Douglass's other choice lies in Eurocentric concepts of self, God, and masculine violence. In my view, the binaries, even if clearly presented, can't be boiled down to Douglass's choice to take the root. What Gilroy misses is that Douglass does not explicitly commit one way or the other: Douglass has it both ways; in both texts he chooses the root but makes it appear like it is only because his friend implored him to do so. Douglass uses both Christian faith and the root, and yet he fully claims neither as the source of his spiritual triumph.

Doubling and multiplying implications generate instability and questions about the relations among Douglass, Sandy, and the root. Is Douglass a devout Christian who also believes in roots? Is Sandy a person of African magic powers that claims to follow the Sabbath? If Sandy is praised for kindness, what community values the root work that he does? The text expresses and withholds which of these figures values what and for what purposes, while Douglass's story all the while stresses the significance of both Sandy and the root. *Narrative* and *My Bondage* together affirm and deny, validate and undermine the crucial questions about Douglass, Sandy, and their beliefs about the status of roots.

Sandy is a medicine man, a root worker who helps show that slave religion, exemplary homosocial bonds, and good Samaritanism can be read as singular or simultaneous and need not be defined by moving for or against freedom. Sandy is both periphery and center, incidental acquaintance and community leader of wisdom and trust. Douglass, Sandy, and the root's doublings offer windows into enslaved Africans' social life and full range of choices, thoughts, rituals, and daily practice. The 1845 and 1855 texts read together show how Douglass presents himself and Sandy during the same historical event from different points of view. If the root is not forgotten but tested and validated, as in 1845, and then reaffirmed in its importance by Douglass's dismissal of it in 1855, the root remains central to Douglass's self. The root episode transforms Douglass's self into an ongoing self-problematic committed to coexisting points of view. Destabilizing Douglass via the root unsettles all other selves and objects as well as how Douglass relates to them while simultaneously doubling down on the root's significance.

After defeating Covey, Douglass declares: "however I might remain a slave in form, the day had passed forever when I could be slave in fact."[21] The root is an object that reminds Douglass that he will never be whipped, and it troubles the stability and certainty of Douglass's self and relation to others. Douglass's famous words about the form/fact of slavery also bear out in this layered dynamic. The slave in form refers to Douglass's acting like an obedient slave; yet while appearing like an obedient slave he can never be a slave in fact. This is paradoxical because he is a slave. But his perception of himself elides the complicit slave. The willing slave is a lie, and in telling a lie for others to believe, he seizes ownership of the narrative because on the inside he plots; his interior is his to express or withhold.[22] Douglass's exterior performance is not fake; both form and fact are authentic enough to be believable to Douglass and to the people he interacts with. In this way, both the slave in form and the slave in fact are true, opposed, and simultaneous.

Douglass's performance for his masters and other members of his slave community substantiates multiple selves, outlooks, and sets of meaning made possible by the fact of "epistemic estrangement" between subjects, what cannot be known as well as what can be known about them.[23] The slave form/fact opposition is counterlife because through it I see proliferating dialectics for investigation, discovery, and argument. The slave form/fact opposition is the culmination of what the root moment signifies, the gap between appearance and reality; put together and sustained throughout without reconciliation, Douglass's figuring and performance, institutional disciplining and self-authenticity, produce an ongoing self-problematic that substantiates the occasion for visiting and revisiting Douglass's varied selves.

Alice Night

Alice Night, from Edward Jones's *The Known World* (2004), is a slave. Unlike the very real historical and literary Douglass, Alice is Jones's fictional fabrication. She wanders the Townsend plantation as a madwoman who does things no one can really make sense of. Part of the reason Douglass needs the root is that Covey's vocation was to learn, to know, to figure Douglass, to make him an obedient, submissive slave. Covey can't figure the root and his overconfidence prevents him from realizing that Douglass is capable of subjecting him to Douglass's actions. In Jones's novel, everyone who is not Alice is more like Covey, believing she is understandable as mentally ill and insignificant. Most of the characters have no idea that Alice is performing the slave "in form" throughout the entire novel except for the Black overseer Moses (who guesses).

This purposefully misleading characterization bears the weight of the novel's title. While the novel focuses quite squarely on the Black slave owner Henry Townsend, a figure underrepresented and unknown, it is Alice, more than any other character, who obliterates the sociological and historical certainty of assessing slave behavior and motivation in the book. Alice escapes, leads other slaves to freedom, owns property in a Black community, and composes unimaginable art. By novel's end Alice epitomizes what Douglass's root provokes about what we can know about slave subjects, that subjects who need to be known for labor may upend knowable social relations between subjects. The discovered uncertainty and unreliability of who Alice is converts immediate truth into a multiplicity of questions—some answerable and most unanswerable. This is where the heart of Alice's counterlife rests. Alice is an amalgamation, a repository and producer of slave social being. She symbolizes a loose thread, which, once pulled, unravels conventional historical understanding and narrative expectations that we rely on to produce and reveal the social worlds of slavery. This forceful unraveling delivers *Known World*'s counterlife.

What no one can deny about *The Known World* is the masterful treatment of truth. All writers have some version of this, but the science of archival records in the novel connotes the confidence of verification, an affirmative answer to whether the novel is based on true events. Jones insists he wanted the reader to feel and know Manchester County, Virginia, as a real place with census records and historians who debated its social, economic, and political conditions.[24] Jones's methods to verify a complete fabrication contribute to that sense of reality, and what is possible is strikingly more powerful than a novel about incarnated ghosts or someone who attains myth in Morrison's historical universe. This is not to say that Jones does not thread the needle between what is possible and what is not, what can be known and what can't, but Alice is key; she achieves something we cannot imagine for herself or ourselves.

Alice comes across as just another interesting figure on the plantation. She first excites interest because she watches Moses pleasuring himself. Moses, the plantation overseer, was annoyed but not surprised by her antics. Alice does odd things like singing nonsensical songs, wandering aimlessly (seemingly so) at night, and agitating the slave watchers. Jones raises the stakes of Alice's identity when Moses sends his family off with her to escape. Priscilla, Moses's wife, asks what proves to be a basic but profound question: "What is Alice, Moses? What is she? . . . What can Alice do?" And Moses replies, "She knows more than you think. . . . Just trust Alice to know what to do."[25] Moses tells Alice he knows why she's been roaming the outskirts of the plantation; though she refuses to let on, Moses knows what she has been up to. The reader cannot be sure of Moses's knowledge and confidence because he wants his family out of the way so he can sleep in the master's house with the widowed Caldonia Townsend. Moses could be sending his own family to certain death or to be recaptured and sold. How much he may or may not actually know about Alice is part of the way the reader views Moses's moral calculus. Hence, we have this glimpse of partial evidence and suspicion that is crystal clear after we find out that Alice escaped with Priscilla. Nevertheless, even if the reader did suspect that Moses was correct about his suspicion of Alice's plans, he or she can have no clue of the real depth that Alice withholds.

Jones's obscurity with Alice's history, social interactions, and interiority, paradoxically, begins with a precise set of facts around Alice that make her understandable and viable as a character. Alice, like other slaves, was sold as a commodity for the purpose of working. Henry Townsend brags about what a deal he got on her. The rumor is that she got kicked in the head by a mule, which caused her erratic behavior. Whether that is true is irrelevant. The fact of the matter is that Alice labored well, at least well enough that her consistency gave her value. This is no simple fact. Alice's existence as a valuable commodity who did her job consistently and effectively is equally important, although not as initially interesting, as the fact of a Black slave owner in the South. This means that her materiality, her viability as a producer of goods, constitutes her social relations.

The other more notable aspect of her personality is the appearance of mental illness. Alice appears to be out of her mind: "Alice, the woman without a mind . . . had started going about the land in the night, singing and talking to herself and doing things that sometimes made the hair on the backs of the slave patrollers' necks stand up"; they "got used to seeing Alice wander about and she became just another fixture in the patrollers' night."[26] The slave catchers bring her back to the master repeatedly because of her wandering. She grabbed the crotches of slave catchers, flipped up her frock, and at the death of her master she sang songs with irreverence.

What makes sense is that because she worked so well master Henry never sold her and ordered her returned when found by slave catchers. What makes less sense is how she could work so well and then be so odd in her behavior. It seems that no one asked why communal labor consistently did not provoke questions about her otherwise unpredictable antics. This is what only Moses appears to catch but does not relay to the reader. One night Moses follows her to the edge of the plantation, and he admits that he knows what she is doing.[27] Alice says to him, "I don't know about goin nowhere. . . . I'm just Alice on Marse Henry's plantation, thas all I know."[28] Moses says, "She knows more than you think, woman. She does."[29]

From the end of the novel, we know that Alice was lying and that Moses's intuition was right. The point here is that Jones is overlapping the consistency and certainty of material production with the inconsistency and unreliability of mental illness and the notion that the significance of being a good slave granted her freedom to test limits. When one asks, Who is Alice Night?, rather than answer, An enslaved woman pretending to be erratic, we see two compelling realities both simultaneous and real. Alice's knowing how to be as important as she was but also how to be what Douglass called a "slave in form" points back to the idea that the people who closely observed her, who knew her, were completely wrong about her. Calvin's letter amplifies this, particularly with his emphasis on Alice's art and not the fact that it is miraculous that they were there, intact and running the very community he wanted to be a part of. Before we get to Alice as artist, her persona and social relations already combined contrasting aspects: material and immaterial, certainty and uncertainty, historical clarity and absence of facts, all of which operate without resolution. Her labor originates a scene of materiality that multiplies into the enigma that Alice is. But rather than revealing the depth of Alice, her real thought process, and her history, we see her overwhelming artistry through Calvin's bewilderment.

In a letter Calvin directs the reader's attention to the first of two works he calls miracles.[30] Calvin discovers a huge room filled with tables for dining, but no one was dining; instead visiting people stopped to view this "enormous wall hanging":

> a grand piece of art that is part tapestry, part painting, and part clay structure all in one exquisite Creation, hanging silent and yet songful on the Eastern wall. It is . . . a kind of map of life of the County Manchester, Virginia. But a "map" is such a poor word for such a wondrous thing. It is a map of life made with *every kind of art man has ever thought to represent himself.* Yes, clay. Yes, paint. Yes, cloth. There are no people on this "map," just all the houses and barns and roads and cemeteries and wells in our Manchester. It is what God sees when He looks down on Manchester. At the bottom right-hand corner of this Creation there were but two stitched words. Alice Night.[31]

Alice produces a recognizable and cogent map of all the material objects, structures, and geography for the entirety of Manchester County. A photographic replication suggests a realist painting or a snapshot. Jones makes an object like a map, to be read, to be understood, and he then unravels that entire notion. This suggests that Alice's mindless wandering was quite mindful, of structure and the complete layout of county, a gesture toward the total mastery of material, space, geography, and history—material foundations perfected as if in spiritual terms, a flash of insight. But it is an art installation that is as defiant as the artist, suggesting a technical execution that exceeds the medium by militating against hierarchies of technique: Alice appears as a vessel for God's view, and this map is her "songful" personal point.

Jones continues to depict what Calvin sees in Alice's own work with comprehensiveness and fullness. The map of life, which had no animated life in it, was outdone by another of Alice's artworks. Jones emphasizes stunning detail, capaciousness, and multidimensionality in this passage:

> This one is about your home, Caldonia. It is your plantation, and again, it is what God sees when He looks down. There is nothing missing, not a cabin, not a barn, not a chicken, not a horse. Not a single person is missing. I suspect that if I were to count blades of grass, the number would be correct as it was once when the creator

of this work knew that world. And again, in the bottom right-hand corner are the stitched words "Alice Night."[32]

There is impeccable detail down to blades of grass. All life: here the whole is all there, but it is entirely localized to the Townsend plantation. This plantation comprises a vision that shatters boundaries. How can a single person capture such diversity? How can a fragment capture the whole?

Viewing it, Calvin writes, he suspects that if "I were to count the blades of grass, the number would be correct as it was once when the creator of this work knew that world."[33] The phrase "knew that world" is a red flag. The work of art that has Calvin in disbelief, even before he knew the artist, is said to be miraculous for its detail. The creations are what "God sees when He looks down." Perhaps this is hyperbolic, but what Calvin witnesses is the impossible made possible, the culminating logic of the book founded in the anomaly of the Black slaveholder in white supremacist slaveholding Virginia. Alice captures the Townsend plantation and the geography of Manchester County, without anything missing. This perfection is a photographic mirror, a replica of knowledge. Alice knows the world and reproduces it without error. Is this *truth*? Is it the knowable truth as historicity emanating from the expression of the person we know the least about? How is this unfathomable "all" produced by an individual, a fragment?

Jones's deployment of Calvin's letter is a device. It is as if the audience is watching Calvin look at the mesmerizing scene. Calvin stands transfixed; the letter is memory that the audience relives through Calvin's description. Thus, the audience borrows Calvin's eyes in remembering the people, space, time, and history of the novel, and not just those Calvin is aware of but even more: as "there are matters in my memory that I did not know were there until I saw them on the wall."[34] There is more and more in Alice's work. It is abundant beyond his imagination. Calvin himself cannot transmute the beauty that overwhelms him. He sinks to his knees. The letter recalls how this chapter begins. Calvin anticipates that he hopes to find "Life in this city, more life than his Soul can contain."[35] The sinking to his knees indicates not just beauty but the sublime effect of Alice's work on him. Calvin, member of the master class, submits to the event created by a former slave on his sister's plantation. There are facts that cannot be denied here. Alice is now free, and Calvin submits to the experience created by Alice's work but comes to terms with the desire to belong to the community she heads.

What is stunning about Alice's creation is that bifurcation affects Calvin. He is an outsider who wants inclusion, place, community. The power of creation reverberates in the transfixed present, but it only does so as itself, as the past, as something distinctive and invented by someone who had miraculously come through it only to reinvent it, revere it through art. The life that Calvin finds in Alice's work is not just hers but is new. We are beyond the master/slave binary already. Jones's ending to *The Known World* pushes beyond tractable knowledge and fields of instruments and into the realm of feeling, perception, and realization.

Calvin writes about Alice: "Whatever she had been in Virginia, she was that no more."[36] The mentally challenged, erratic laborer was now artist, property owner, and community leader. The dynamic change of these titles is quite literal because she could not have been these things in Virginia on the Townsend plantation. Yet, what she was refers to Priscilla's question, "What is Alice?" What Alice is—who she is, her work, and the dramatic effect that work has on Calvin—culminates at the end, and Jones insists on no declarative answer and no way to answer it. But this contradicts or renders superficial Calvin's observance of the difference between Alice in Virginia and Alice now. Jones moves across boundaries of slavery and freedom not to declare one the ultimate victor but to reiterate Alice's elusiveness and what Calvin has found through her: "more life."

The power of Jones's assemblages of history, texture, time, and social relations is that some of the critical questions of agency have gone assumed. How did she do it? What books she read and what schemes of power she instrumentalized on her behalf throughout their journey to freedom are invisible to us and will not be known. Alice is radical for the historical and aesthetic effect she produces, how little we know, want to know, and can't know. Morally, Alice did a great thing by helping Priscilla and Celeste to freedom, and she maintains property where Black folks gather and feel welcome, but Jones does not emphasize Alice's heralding moral sacrifice. Jones reveals how the radical and exciting exceeding of boundaries of knowledge produces magnificent art. Alice: maker of the artistic creation of slavery's world that transfixes us and is sublime in its articulation of historical truth's ineffability.

Alice is powerfully enigmatic through and through. Alice is not just an enigma for who she is; her sanity alerts us to the thriving enigma of subjectivity and its ongoing and unrelenting presence in social life. Alice wears a number of colliding and coalescing hats that make it hard to discern if freedom's political valence gives her a new self or an old self or what corresponding institutional structures and social attachments disturb all of them—whether or not a closed or open system produced Alice. We can make neither heads nor tails of her, and that generates her manifold impact as an exemplifier of counterlife.

Memory as Medicine

Douglass's Sandy was a medicine man. I read Douglass as a trickster, obscurer, and clarifier of both self and social relations. Alice of *The Known World* diversifies and deepens this playful trickery to perfection. Alice was a trickster who mediated the trickster in all of us through artistic impressions of historical and sociological fact. Here, I focus on the art of Radcliffe Bailey, a living artist in whose installations slavery is a central theme. The only published book of his art is *Memory as Medicine* (2011). He also calls his own artist persona a trickster, which puts him in great company with my reading of Douglass and Jones. Bailey sees his work as medicine and as therapy.[37] But what is medical therapy for himself, his audience, Black people, or anyone who sees, listens to, and experiences his installations? Medicinal healers like Sandy and contemporary physicians prescribe a mix of elixirs, roots, and pills. Caring healers treat people to alleviate their pain and ailments. Bailey insists that memory itself is medicine. For Bailey, memory is inspiration from history, experiences, scientific discovery, and art of all kinds—anything from his explorations that he recalls, which explains the elaborate incoherence in his creative and diverse expression.[38] Bailey's embrace of memory's imprecision and unexpectedness challenges anyone to locate his radical imagination in a singular set of political terms for an explicit greater good. Counterlife lies in Bailey's work's implicit refusal to recognize a discernable target of self-revelation, epistemic confirmation, or political resolution.

Bailey's art, moreover, does not even identify what in fact needs therapy; when it comes to slavery's traumas, what, if anything, can memories heal? Do we need to remember slavery or forget it, get over it through tools and rituals of remembrance, or should we confront slavery, be willing to go wherever that confrontation goes, and understand that facing it could be many things all at once? Neither option satisfies Bailey and his art installations. Bailey creates images of slave pins from Gorée Island, ships from the Middle Passage, and stories of slaves from his family, and these invoked creations repeatedly militate against our expectations until one does not know the difference between historical fact and the sublime fantasy of inhabiting historicity's aesthetic.

Bailey mixes painting, sculpture, collage, and other media and genres to reinvent Black diasporic geographies. West Africa and the Americas appear in his work quite literally in maps or historical places with specific links to Bailey's DNA. Bailey traces his ancestors to Sierra Leone and Guinea. Bailey's use of space is inspiring, profound, and sometimes just downright overwhelming. One does not just view his art. His artwork creates encounters and reencounters without consistent media, materials, and forms. In such an encounter one sees music notes and hears the actual sounds of John Coltrane and Sun Ra. Bailey toys and frustrates time, space, history, and ready-made connections with social and biographical attachments. Bailey's arresting refusals turn the insurgent grounds of political possibility into immovable sludge. Political artifacts without utility, slavery's guises of death cast in spring's music and color, and mystifications between an individual's past and the collective present become perfectly and wondrously realized. This is the profound cost of slavery's sublime illumination in Bailey's installations. Slavery is sometimes Bailey's focus, as a historical echo, a point of departure, or as nameless individuals on the Middle Passage. The Middle Passage, more specifically, does not appear by itself but is constellated and collected with other stories that speak to alienation, loss, the space of awe, respect, and fear of the ocean.

Manthia Diawara revels in the "rhizomatic quality" of Bailey's paintings and installations.[39] Diawara points to Bailey's lateral shoots, adventitious roots, and flowing connections of time, space, memory, history, and materials. Diawara calls these layers "rigorously political,"[40] yet he does not elucidate what kind of political rigor he means in his writing on Bailey. Bailey takes cultural icons, famous historical places and moments, family heirlooms, and moments in the political geography of Black radicalism, and he re-creates them in such a way that simultaneously loses their political utility and intensifies the force of irreverence. And thus, I would amend Diawara's assessment from "rigorously political" to something akin to rigorously radical with the understanding that Bailey's work challenges how we grasp Black subjects.

What we see in Bailey's installation is what Huey Copeland analyzes and studies in Black art installations that feature slavery. Copeland does not discuss Bailey in *Bound to Appear* (2013), but his writing about Glenn Ligon and others is pertinent. Copeland claims there "is a complex dialectic between fact and fiction, presence and absence, subject and object, sound and image, free play and determination," and in Ligon's work we may not know what "it is like to be a slave now . . . but we can see what it means to be a subject now."[41] Copeland sees this subjectivity in slave installations as part of a "visual politics of conversion," which is a "coming to grips with those practices that have undergirded the production of black being."[42]

Copeland is right to recognize the dialectical movement of "fact and fiction," but he overlooks the conundrum he proposes between a politics of conversion and what he suggests as an ongoing vacillation between "presence and absence" and so on. Conversion means moving from something to another thing, a constitutive change that is meaningful because it is sustained. If the conversion was one in constant motion and vacillation, that dynamic undermines any meaningful new reality or position. So, it would be helpful here if Copeland would elaborate the grounds and stakes of conversion. How does one convert or transform from something to something else if one is locked in complex dialectics? Does the subject we can see appear with an absolute identity or in the conflict of fugitive versus trickster? I'm willing to accept that complex dialectics operate in the work of Bailey, Ligon, Kara Walker, and other slave text installations, but my contention here is that a formidable disruption frustrates what politics one is being transformed from and to. The slave text doubles back to the art experience itself, the artist, and the one who witnesses it is like Calvin from *The Known World*, "transfixed." If one turns away, even for a minute, from the traction of political conversion and turns toward encountering art objects' rhizomatic quality, then the experiences of art can challenge and disturb the political clarity or progressive traction we too often seek.

Bailey's *Notes from Elmina I* portrays the slave castles in Ghana. The painting consists mostly of ocean and grassland that breaks into beach and the infamous fortress. Bailey limns the entire scene in wonderful color: blues, yellow, green, touches of orange. Sky, water and color, gold and yellow recast back on the castle so even the castle's creamy white shimmers gold. The land is green, lush, and minty. Mint green is a mark of Bailey's grandfather and trails of ancestry.[43]

On first glance, one might think the Elmina fortress is a tropical vacation escape. In some sense, given the slave tourism industry, it is. Moreover, what unites every inch of vast water and sky and small land is sheet music of European classical music. Bailey's painting of the slave castle cap-

FIGURE 2.1 Radcliffe Bailey, *Notes from Elmina I*, 2010. © Radcliffe Bailey.
Courtesy of the artist and Jack Shainman Gallery, New York.

tures wonder, pleasure, and escape, and yet, as Kimberly Juanita Brown has observed, the art "highlights death's proximity, its unmistakable intimacy."[44] How does the place of torn flesh, separated families, rape, kidnapping, and the most wicked psychological violence the western world has recorded come to be like something in a dream—a place that compels you to revisit?

Bailey's interlacing of music in *Elmina I* is key. His perspective in this painting is a constant figuring of distance and intimacy, and strokes of classical music lay open the pathway for meditative experiential viewing that permits proximity without devastation. It reminds me of Toni Morrison's *Beloved* (1987), where Amy sang, told stories, and talked over Sethe's whipped back. She sang for both of them. She had to address the wounds, the spirits, and effect overall, and the fact that Sethe was on the verge of death. Amy used the song and antics of humor to ameliorate the strangeness, danger, and urgency of her encounter with Sethe.[45]

The music in Bailey's painting is classical, which is a historical event in its splendor and ferocity, a return to the event. The blue waves interrupted by music and the spectacle of the castle announces that this is not the moment of violent trauma but an artistic return where there can be beauty now where there was not. Bailey's painting forces us to wonder whether there is a beauty in refreshing and awakening historical consciousness. There is, but the sublime affect relies on a cultivated abstraction of horror and exploitation—one refracted through Bailey's lens as one revisits it as an onlooker.

Saidiya Hartman traveled to Elmina. She visited the castle in its quotidian reality. The "prosaic conduct of everyday life" incensed and perplexed her.[46] There was no reverence for the dead and for the violations that were repeated there. The transactional numbness buried what needs to be seen, discussed, debated, and memorialized by people walking Elmina's grounds. Bailey also visited Elmina. He recalls it as a place he holds in great reverence and splendor but one that maintains a veiled violence.[47]

Diawara calls this vitally strong sense of ongoing contradiction in Bailey's work an "imaginary real of relationships":[48] beauty/ugliness, classical sounds/shrieks of beaten Black bodies, psychological storms of torment/oceanic scenes. Bailey does not aim for realist verisimilitude. The music notes in *Elmina I* call our attention to the tragic graces of history, and mint green marks connect Bailey's family and the present to history's memory. This is Bailey's persona at work: his mysterious configuration of the painting's dimensions lure and bewilder the audience into the fact of the trick; Bailey's trick is the experience of tragedy and suffering with bright spring color layered in. The art informs, tantalizes, and devours as it overwhelms. This experience of looking epitomizes Bailey's belief that "sometimes you [audience members] use your imagination, sometimes your imagination uses you."[49]

The *Windward Coast* is a Middle Passage installation that literalizes music in ways no one would expect. There are no painted notes from classical sheet music as in *Elmina I*, but there are a flurry of piano keys—those of more than four hundred pianos. Bailey records the sound of him dropping the families of piano keys and then replays them through a conch shell on the wall during the exhibit. Bailey creates the installation differently every time, but with the same features: piano keys, a conch shell on the wall, a sparkling bust of a Black man's head. The piano keys have the visual effect of waves and endless sea. Bailey says it reminds him of the view from his grandfather's small boat from shore. Beyond his own vision of smallness in a roving sea, Bailey says he feels even smaller in a vast world and imagines a distant universe.[50] These feelings amalgamate with the most distinctive layer: the figure surrounded by endless piano keys. The sparkling black head looks like one visible African in an ocean of deadwood.

Bailey deploys the singular object of the black head to continue to toy with distance, seeing and being seen. He looks back at each witness and incorporates the modern witness into history's complicity with the past. We witness him in the distance, or he sees us, and this mutual recognition binds the present and past as much as it distinguishes it through the history of missing Africans. Sound accompanies the visual effect. Bailey rarely places the conch shell in the same place. He alerts his viewer to the clanking keys from different aspects. The shell amplifies the prerecorded sounds. As Bailey layers the piano keys he cannot hear how the keys fall to the ground as he drops them. While he drops the keys, he listens to sporadic rhythms of John Coltrane in his headphones. The sound fills the room, and the room is made of piano keys that now make different sounds.

What is Bailey asking his audience to come to grips with as they are disrupted, overwhelmed, and taken over? When one feels small, then big and expansive, one sees and thinks horror and then drowns in the power of music or the distraction of seemingly random key clanging. The physicality of the object demands attention, but the attention lures one into the roving keys, overlapping time, and endless space, outside the grasp of history. How does anything, object or subject, hold one's place while expanding and reproducing yet returning and leaving, becoming many and then

FIGURE 2.2 Radcliffe Bailey, *Windward Coast*, 2009–18. © Radcliffe Bailey.
Courtesy of the artist and Jack Shainman Gallery, New York.

returning back to one again? The subject losing and forgetting himself/
herself/themselves, embodied/disembodied, jolted/comforted asks what
is being recovered or confronted here from invoking the Middle Passage
history or being historical in this way about the Middle Passage. This is
part of what Bailey's haunting power of creation visits on us. The power
of this piece reveals a fantastical confrontation with an imagined reality
of dead lingering slaves at sea and a historical reality that gives the audience a window into tragic and traumatic experience. Slavery comes across
as significant but diffuse, indubitable history but surreal, massive in scope
yet frighteningly individualized.

Bailey's *Returnal* (2007) was inspired by the "door of no return" in Sen-
egal. It is a long pathway, a single doorway that opens to the ocean. It is
a dramatic scene and a terrifying one. The door is ending, negation, the
imagined and real trauma of that historical reality. It is a place remembered for the story of commerce and degradation and for the feeling of
powerlessness to change the historical event of separating family members
from one another and from Africa.

FIGURE 2.3 Radcliffe Bailey, *Returnal*, 2007. © Radcliffe Bailey. Courtesy of the artist and Jack Shainman Gallery, New York.

Bailey takes the concept of his beginnings and endings into his creation of the door. *Returnal* looks like a door of no return in a literal sense; rather than see the ocean through the door, one sees an angel or Christ figure like a constellation in a starry sky. The title *Returnal* suggests infinite return or returning eternally. Bailey produces a continuum that obliterates a conventional sense of time and merges mortality with immortality, holy with unholy, inhumane with humane. In yet another iteration of the door, Bailey focuses on a live dancer in a video vanishing into smoke as if the beauty of life performed came to die in this memorialized place. Bailey unapologetically makes art emotionally moving in its horror and its beauty.

In her book *In the Wake*, Christina Sharpe examines two slavery installations as counters to each other: one is Rodney Leon's *The Ark of Return* (2015), and the other is Charles Gaines's *Moving Chains* (2015). According to Leon, his architectural installation uses the language of spiritual return because physical return to that moment is not possible; the installation serves as a gathering place of "spiritual and emotional transformation, . . . where humanity comes closer together." Leon believes the Ark produces opportunities for "counter-narrative" that can undo some of that experience.[51] Skeptical of Leon's claims, Sharpe asks, "What constitutes a counternarrative here? What is the nature of this undoing?" in Leon's *Ark*?[52] Sharpe does not directly answer these questions herself, and she indicates that Leon's *Ark* installation has no specific answers that point to the counter-narrative and undoing that Leon suggests.

Sharpe does, however, point to another art installation that she claims counters Leon's *Ark*. For Sharpe, Gaines's *Moving Chains* offers an experience that is shiplike, where walking through the various formations of chains will be, in Gaines's words, a "ferocious experience."[53] Sharpe emphasizes, "Gaines's visualsonic affective language is not one of pastness and reconciliation" because the "river, that time, that place, are still present," and thus, Gaines's "shiptime" counters the "monumental time" of Leon's *Ark*.[54] The materials and sensorial affects created by Gaines's *Moving Chains* design are undoubtedly different. Gaines's chains are moving, and Gaines imagines the experience to be "a ferocious one." But, for Sharpe, the ferocity Gaines highlights boils down to art being able to communicate affects that cannot be or have yet to be reconciled as well as an ongoing historical present that cannot pass. Sharpe suggests that this is precisely the problem with works like Leon's *Ark*: the past is "pacified in its presentation."[55] But other than "a ferocious experience" the payoff for work keeping the past present remains elusive. Besides countering Leon, what do ferocity, disharmony, and ship time produce in the thousands of people who would walk through this installation on the Mississippi River in St. Louis? It is not clear why *Ark of Return* is materially and affectively at a political disadvantage when compared with Gaines's *Moving Chains* in Sharpe's comparison. I see why the look and sound of moving chains could perhaps chill the spine of an onlooker, but tombs also do so.

What is more, the possible payoff Leon professed about the *Ark* relied on parts of the installation that were tangible and interactive. Leon explains: "We want it to be *very interactive* and we *expect people to touch things* like the map, the image we have of the slave ship and the water."[56] In my view, the spiritual and emotional interactivity will be transformative in Leon's *Ark* and so will walking through Gaines's installation. That's hard to deny. Yet, precisely what peoples' reactions will be and how useful they will be in terms of grappling with slavery's past and present is challenging to say the least. Thinking of these slave texts in terms of remembering/forgetting, past/present, or reconcilable/irreconcilable for political counternarratives assumes a kind of stable affect that these works are resistant to. Sharpe stabilizes and makes political sense of the abstract artistic language and experiences; in doing so she identifies political traction and purposeful awareness. But one cannot prognosticate about what will come out of individuals' experiences of either installation beyond the incredible yet disturbing beauty they produce as aesthetic objects in history.

Wrestling with what is riveting about Leon's tomb, the grating consciousness in Gaines, or the unraveling historical object's affect in Bailey means accepting and sitting with the weight of the enigmatic impact of irreconcilable dialectics. That's their radical power. This radicality becomes its own object, experienced, sometimes overwhelming in fraught and enigmatic affects. Because one cannot tie up any loose ends and pieces of the puzzle move around without culminating in truth, this leaves us undone but also transformed. Thus, the constitutive power that lies in the radical aesthetic force of a contemporary slave text is a transformational power, but this very power undermines turning affect, information, and experience into an immediately usable tool to create political synergy and promote desired outcomes.

Bailey sees medicinal therapy in his art that he never equates fully with reconciling or facing slavery or moving into a definable past-ness. Slavery serves as a vessel for eternity, event, stasis, and movement, where subjects blur into objects or nothing, then everything, then again from a different vantage point. There is indeed slavery in complex dialectics, as Huey Copeland professed, or an affective force distilled and sustained as present, as in Sharpe. This magnificence relishes in artists' rebuff of traditional goals and framing of questions about agents, fugitives, and unfreedom. Bailey encourages us to think of his memory as medicine, as therapy for questions and wounds we rediscover in different ways or realize they were not what we thought they were. His litany of colors, materials, fact, and memory asks us to confront slavery in a vulnerable position that unwinds and diminishes and edifies at the same time.

This thoroughgoing simultaneity defines Bailey's counterlife. Bailey's commitment to traditional objects of Black culture, political events, slavery, blues, jazz, spirituals, and everyday forgotten places and people countering in the realization of slavery becomes a vessel of an imaginative historical scope. Bailey has historical fixity, naming recognizable objects with universal recognition. He feels and revels in the spirit dimension and has forced himself to end seven layers/thoughts, but different every time, and this difference every time is the promise of art. He is a spiritual listener and even a wise man: resetting, probing, and questioning.

The counterlife in Bailey's installations, Douglass's root, and Alice's art and unknown life demonstrates the aesthetic and philosophical force of slavery. These texts assert truth and historical specificity and imply dynamics of liberation, but they also unravel conventional approaches to what truth is, what it means to be historical, and what counts as being radical. Turning back to Ellison can be useful here. He insists that scholars and writers consider the chaotic, vibrant, and "imperious mind" within all subjects, which he considers to be a "mysterious configuration of forces."[57] Bailey, Douglass, and Alice show how slave texts deliver this. Incorporating the psychological and social fact of unwieldiness is a crucial part of history and of thinking historically about the minds and worlds of slaves; doing so unmoors frames and opens up space to listen, imagine, create, and debate.

3

SOUNDS OF BLACKNESS

Then, history becomes a garment we can wear,
and share, and not a cloak in which to hide.
—James Baldwin, "Of the Sorrow Songs"

When singing spirituals, individuals often form a congregation to share a song, but what the individual has in mind when they riff, chorally align, or shout is always, in some part, their own to express, withhold, or change. Like Bailey's installations, spirituals begin with a commitment to history, social conflict, community, and spiritual events, but the disruptive raptures of sound and elevated repetitions loosen all boundaries to categories, points of view, and identity itself. This chapter explores how the counterlife in slaves' spirituals, the ur-sound of Blackness, creates radical newness in a dance with God. Inasmuch as the songs contain and reinvent social conflict, history, and self-transformation, they are equally committed to improvisation, unforeseen revision, and enigmatic instabilities that cannot be predicted or assimilated.

Contradiction defines the counterlife that spirituals make available—a sense of vibrant mutuality that makes subject/object distinctions unreliable. Sterling Brown, reflecting on changes in spirituals' expression from enslavement through the Great Migration, wrote: "What may come of it, if anything, is unpredictable, but so far the vigor of the creative impulse has not been snapped, not even in the slums."[1] It is this ontological character, the "creative impulse," located in the songs, revised over generations, that disturbs and exceeds our ethnographic and epistemological expertise, demanding a new query into this form of musical expression.

Beyond Objects?

Whether as slaves, sharecroppers, leased convicts, or victims of prison pipelines and police brutality, are Black people objects of white dominance? While some scholars may emphatically say yes, others may argue that it depends on perspective and context. Abolitionists agreed that to be a slave was to be a thing or an object solely for a white master's use.[2] Slavery is the sine qua non for objectification. Hortense Spillers argues that New World slavery began not in personhood but in a "zero degree of social conceptualization."[3] Spillers continues: "the ruling episteme that releases the dynamics of naming and valuation" destabilizes Blacks' connection to human personality, cultural institutions, and interpersonal relationships.[4] The overall effect of this separation, according to Spillers, is "total objectification."[5] When one occupies the object position, it means this person is the instrument of whites or another vessel of institutional power that takes away, ignores, or wholly coerces the Black subject's sense of person.

Critics have focused too narrowly on assessing slavery's art forms through the scope of how characters, images, and persons attempt, succeed, or fail to reclaim their agency against regimes of power historically controlled by whites. Through this lens, critics analyze how Blacks discover and recover true self-consciousness for the politics of freedom from an original position of being objectified. Slaves either become subjects or self-conscious resisting objects or drown in overlapping layers of objectification. Perhaps objects, objects to subjects, is not the best way to approach the slave in art or the art that slaves perform. What do we miss about the art of enslaved Africans or representations of it when the slave's objectification by whites determines our thinking? In this chapter, I will turn to the spirituals that slaves created to consider how we conceptualize the songs we call spirituals and how thinking about them in a different light can transform approaches to the art and social life of enslaved Africans beyond objects and subjects.

Reflecting on the long history of Black music, James Baldwin imagines the source of the spirituals in the moments enslaved Africans were placed on auction blocks across the Americas. Baldwin explains: "This music begins on the auction block." "The auction block," he continues, "is the demolition, by Europe, of all human standards."[6] What are the human standards being demolished? Whites rob Africans of voice, dignity, and choices over their own life and any semblance of equality and human decency. Given that human beings are not strangers to treating one another with abrasive cruelty, either within families or from other tribes, nations, and creeds, what Baldwin alludes to when he refers to standards is more of a spiritual and political ideal of human praxis; the auction block is the destruction of the ideal social contract and American democratic family—demolished and debased. The auction block, where auctioneers call for the price of an individual person, commodifies the African, a process that enacts property rights and severe social and political exclusion—the slave is an object for his or her master, of a broader slaveholding regime of whites, and of someone else's historical narrative and philosophical disposition. To return to Baldwin, then, the music begins in the physical and psychological violence of the auctioning of slaves; the origins of the first American art form in our modern democracy begin in the objectification of enslaved Africans.

Hearing the song "No More Auction Block for Me," Fred Moten might say that to compose, to sing, to utter, to perform, in that remembrance of iconographic subjection, verifies that, indeed, objects can and do resist.[7] Decades of work on Black culture, before and after Moten, see the origins and creation of spirituals as evidence of Black cultural resistance in slavery, in spite of objectification; the songs evidence oppositional culture, the claiming or seizing of subjectivity through the very scene of debasement. Other scholars see spirituals as evidence of the creative musical and performative talents of slaves but not evidence of a latent or direct oppositional culture—suggesting that singing for, against, or under the direction of whites further ensnares slaves in the tentacles of slavery's grip; expressing oneself through song captures the illusion of subjectivity but actually further indebts the African to slave masters' schemes of objectification.

The scholarship on spirituals, from musicologists to historians and poets interested in Black culture, varies. Scholars debate whether spirituals were a mere parroting of white Protestant hymns or were composed originally by slaves; to what degree the performance, content, and arrangement are derived from West African religious life and music; whether spirituals are sophisticated and cerebral and complex, coded to trick or mislead whites, or simple and purely affective; and whether the songs are calls for organizing disruption, revolts, and runaways or praises to passively endure the present and wait for the afterlife. I am moving across decades of arguments with various political backdrops. For different reasons, since the turn of the twentieth century, scholars, politicians, and artists have demonstrated the unique and sophisticated contributions of Black people, enslaved and free, to Western culture in order to garner equal treatment in academic institutions in the United States and in the modern world generally. In this vein, the vital thread through much scholarship on spirituals is that Black slaves were in fact agential subjects, engineers and originators of the spirituals and not objects or pawns of white influence, language, and performative techniques. Far beyond what I discuss here, for generations spirituals and the varieties of Black music they've spawned have been pivotal in projecting Black humanity beyond the horizon of marginalization and social inequality.

At this juncture, what is more interesting to me is how the study of the origins and the importance of how slaves performed "Steal Away," "Go Down, Moses," "Been in the Storm Too Long," or "We Are Climbing Jacob's Ladder" is wide and varied, yet the overall frames of discussion aim at identifying the role Black religious and musical expression serves as actual or symbolic political utility or how the spirituals forge the foundations of a Black radical tradition. This brings coherency and clarity to what kinds of questions we ask about spirituals and why they are important to us intellectually and politically.

Do frames like object to subject, inhuman to human, nonperson to person, limit what we're asking of the spirituals and oversimplify the social life, conflict, and imaginative sourcing of the slaves that generated them? In our effort to make sense of spirituals as distinctively African, African American, political and not passive, coded and not direct, complex and not simple, have scholars delimited how we study the archives of slaves' singing? By mounting a defense of the force and originality of spirituals in a variety of historical and political contexts, what have we missed properly attending to?

Part of the inspiration for this chapter comes from my reading of Zora Neale Hurston's essay "Spirituals and Neo-Spirituals" and James Weldon Johnson's poem "O Black and Unknown Bards" and listening to the concepts of Bernice Johnson Reagon about the singing of spirituals.[8] Hurston emphasizes spontaneity; the improvisation of shouts, calls, and moans; and the radical variations that are always incomplete and ongoing. Johnson believes that the spirituals demonstrate how a slave could own any moment in song; one of the most telling aspects of ethnographic witnesses to slaves singing spirituals is that the performances were passionate, incoherent, and even impenetrable. When Johnson calls the composers of the spirituals "unknown bards" he refers to them as unremembered and unrecorded by history. But I approach spirituals from a different angle by taking the forceful unknowing in the songs quite literally. When a slave owns a moment in communal song, who knows the specific meaning, thought, vision, and value of that ownership besides the person inhabiting the moment? If most spiritual experiences during the singing are beyond words, even the singer may see and feel and hear something forceful without being able to articulate it to others. It is in the simultaneous and irresolvable known/unknown dyad where I demonstrate the counterlife in spirituals. In this chapter I revisit the way the slave's song straddles contradiction; its great coherency of form finds creative force in its partially or fully ungraspable aspects. I submit that we take more seriously the enigmatic aspects of the performed spiritual, and we ought to read and examine and witness spirituals as sites of contradiction, where we see, on the one hand, subjects refusing objectification and, on the other, a performance where subject/object categories break down and lose their cogency and explanatory power.[9]

Bill Brown implies this slave/object construct is a thing relation, but he imagines the slave's thing relation as akin to the thwarting force of an inanimate object being sold alongside a slave like a chair.[10] But what I contend by conceptualizing spiritual singing as a thing relation is not about ontological perception. Neither in law nor outside it are slaves confused for anything but unequal and inferior persons. As I've claimed elsewhere, "Things are not ever confused with persons; there is no ontological scandal on this point and the quotidian register; persons are persons."[11] Thing theory, for my argument here, offers us initially a way outside or through routine questions about whether one's subject status is accepted or recognized and denied or whether one succeeds or fails in resisting one's own objectification. The thingness of persons, as I call it, makes counterlife manifest; it accepts confusion and lack of clarity as part of the pathway to insight, embracing the unknown/known binary, which I think can ultimately refresh our critical perspectives on spirituals and the social life that saw them as a way to provide transformative visions in a chaotic and unfair democracy.

Baldwin says that in spirituals he hears a historical question, an existential aporia: "Who am I? What am I doing here?"[12] How did the slave answer this question if half of the answer comes in moans, groans, and shrieks and is never answered the same way twice? Why did the slave enter the water God is going to trouble? Spirituals give us the opportunity to think about and sustain irreconcilable contradiction at the crux of what it means to be historically, socially, and morally convicted, but the price tag of realizing this opposition is that it shrugs off or calls into question the immediacy of reading the spirituals as ready-made plots toward collective freedom. Seeing the thingness of persons in spirituals reveals counterlife by reopening and resetting how we prioritize and help articulate what slaves, individually and collectively, were committed to, their sense of meaning, value, and purpose.

Objects, Persons, or Things?

William Wells Brown sums up what it means to be a slave when he says, "He is a chattel; he is a thing."[13] To be a thing, in this sense, is to be an object "in the power of the owner"—exposed to every abuse, whether under the guise of encouraging more efficient labor or encouraging submission. The master "can dispose of his wife, dispose of his offspring, and can dispose of everything that belongs to the slave."[14] From abolitionists' point of view, masters have absolute power over the slave; the slave is solely an extension of the master's will. One does not have to look far across abolitionist print culture to find various renditions of Brown's conclusion about being a slave: "the slave has not even himself; he has nothing at all."[15]

One cannot dispute Brown's catalog of violations. But there is some trickery in Brown's presentation. He claims the slave has nothing, but the question is, if the slave indeed has nothing and no interests of his own, then why does the slave not only have wives, children, and social bonds but dread their painful loss? One could say that all these attachments, the joy, heartbreak, choices, are all perfectly choreographed by the disciplinary power of white supremacy, the closed system of ideal mastership, or the necessary and illusive constraints of social death. But these tactics of coercion, if so effective, should also allow for seamless violations—mostly accepted by the slave. The slave would feel minimal violation, and just as master parts with slave so should mother and child. No system, even if slavery was a coherent monolith, has ever been that effective. Moreover, the affective power and moral value of Brown's presentation relies on the fact that there is a powerful sense of violation, and everybody—the slave, the master, and Brown's audience—feels it. For the violation of a slave's person to have significance, the slave has to have one that everyone knows is being violated. This means the slave has a self, wishes, desires, connections, and a way of thinking that manifests personhood, despite being subject to whatever abuses the master sees fit.

In this equation, there are two sets of interests: the master's possession of a slave and Brown's description that a slave has objects that he possesses, enjoys, and uses, which include the people he is closely connected to. How does the master or even slave confirm that the slave is broken and/or selfless? How well does a slave master have to know a slave to break him or her, and how much does the slave learn about the master in the laborious interpersonal contact that occurs between them? How does the master know that the slave is not pretending to be broken to return to more comfortable social arrangements or, better yet, await more opportunities to carry out the slave's interest in covert ways? Breaking is physical and mental, and there is no way to confirm or guarantee this process is ever complete. The slave may happily labor and think tactically about cutting the master's throat even if he or she never does. Hence, contrary to Brown's account that the slave has "not even himself," it is the slave's self that masters engage to protect themselves, or to garner more proficient labor production, or to gain sexual pleasure and power, or to undertake other forms of exploitation. One cannot say that the slave is not taken as a person if he or she as a person is taken into account when masters assess a slave's value and impact on a social community. The person I identify in the slave transcends any legal or economic category. This personhood does not depend on a politically oriented or social consciousness. It may have little or nothing to do with resisting or rising above current laws, labor conditions, or the exchange of commodities.

Recalling Baldwin's words from earlier in this chapter, the cruelest reduction of humanity could be witnessed at a slave auction with its coffles of men and women. The advertisements of slaves alongside the for-sale signs of horses, furniture, and other inanimate objects suggested that the slave was just another product. Auction blocks, slave coffles, and pens where slaves awaited sale contained other stories and active social relations. Slaves relied on information about masters to manipulate their sales.[16] Slaves fabricated themselves to engineer whatever they could for various desired outcomes, especially as it related to keeping family as close as possible.[17] Walter Johnson explains that even in the heart of degradation, the slaves' self-interest thrived in their strategic actions to manipulate the outcomes of their sales.[18] My point here is that total debasement does not evacuate personal self-interest, which individualizes slaves, their experiences, and what they wanted out of their attempts to remake themselves for their own reasons.

In the painting *Slaves Waiting for Sale* (1861), Eyre Crowe provides another example of this. Crowe's painting focuses on the slaves, not the auctioneers or the spectacle of the auction itself.[19] Maurie McInnis contends that Crowe's attention to slaves as individuals was deliberate, to avoid providing just another visual representation of anonymous victims.[20] In that work, Crowe emphasizes that slavery caused the entire conundrum of persons and things. The painting paradoxically indicates the immorality of selling persons as commodity objects, and this immorality relies on conceiving of the victims as persons. *Slaves Waiting for Sale* portrays the slave quarters as a mixture of strangers and known people who have spouses, children, and other family members. One commenter on the painting describes it as "a scene of Southern slave life, bearing internal knowledge of local truth."[21] But what is the internal knowledge they share, and how do they share it and relate to it? The commenter knows they have internal knowledge but only must marvel at the fact of it not being what is actually in the person's head. The painting, then, reiterates that each slave has thoughts, relations, and social attachments—interiority, even—which constitute the "personal" in Crowe's painting. What is equally crucial about the personal is the epistemic and psychological distance between the fact of the internal knowledge and what is and can be expressed. Hence, *Slaves Waiting for Sale* reflects the Stanley Cavell–inspired tautology that a person is taken as a person; the tautology strongly indicates that not knowing what is in someone's head, and the desire to know what cannot be known, also defines the personal.

Igor Kopytoff explains that there is a moment between first capture and first sale where the slave is unambiguously a commodity.[22] Kopytoff goes on to contend that after the slave's sale he or she takes a "new social identity" (so does the master), which is possible, but if "every slave has many biographies," as Kopytoff claims, how does one biography end and the other begin?[23] Slaves are fully evaluated for temperament, duration, and sexual potency, a process that itemizes the slave. This itemization, slave taxonomy, presents a history and pictures. There are undoubtedly layers of biography as well as self-fashioning. I do not see how Kopytoff gets around the social and ontological reality that living beings contain and communicate histories of themselves and that there is no way to establish a zero point of history or a zero point of social existence or personality. Slavery provides the opportunity to point out the fiction that "becoming a slave" or turning a person into a product is not as obvious as the change to a social or legal category that corresponds to it.

Slavery or another oppressive condition asks readers to assume nothing, walk back assumptions and pretexts, and turn social givens into questions in order to reevaluate parameters, thoughts, and experiences of all persons involved in the social conflict. Can slavery begin with the object if the slave is a person? I want to insert the person where object and flesh currently belong to unsettle the trajectory that the object designation implies. As critics and students of Black life in aesthetics, we must be prepared to read texts and subjects as counterlife—as having multiple and layered interests, desires, and affiliations that may have nothing to do with politics or historical trajectories toward revolt and revolution. To do so with enslaved Africans' spirituals provides a vital window onto the full gamut of possibilities of what it means to live.

In the Water . . .

Spirituals are folk songs composed and performed by slaves during work, in religious meetings, for entertainment, or when people had the opportunity to hum or sing. Biblical themes and tropes occupy many spirituals, and other songs that slaves sing have little to no reference to God or the Bible. On a related note, one aspect of spirituals that scholars seem to agonize over is the modern sense of the sacred/secular division that enslaved Africans did not abide by. So, there are songs with ethical and religious tenor that do not mention anything specifically religious, and there are specifically religious songs that allude to actions and thinking clearly outside the domain of the sacred (like the readiness to escape of a group of slaves). The songs cover almost every thinkable aspect of life and explore the existential limits of faith, love, and one's confrontation with earthly finitude. Spirituals performed with various percussive rhythms give way to moans and chants that lead to flashes of spirit possession. When slaves had the opportunity the songs were sung in a circle; the circle's movement forms the depths of familial and ancestral connections to the ongoing greater cosmos and the singers' purpose within it. Spirituals maintained an important role in Black performance from the formation of traveling glee clubs like the Fisk Jubilee Singers, and their early presence in Black film, to the background moans that accompany Black tragedies in contemporary television. Folk singers and gospel singers performed popular renditions of spirituals during radical movements and civil rights organizing.

In songs like "Go Down, Moses," enslaved Africans appropriate biblical myth to make sense of their current suffering. Through the singing of the song, through the sharing of witnesses, members of the circle testify to God's power of deliverance, spiritual transformation, and communal connection. Thus, the despised and abused slaves claim value and dignity through the transformative spirit of song. Thus, the collective and individual battle for identity and self-definition through communal performance saliently begins. The singers reference saints and ancestors who've gone before; their lessons forge ways to interpret and confront social reality—divine revelation and liberation worked hand in hand. The sense of revelation is individual and communal. The community calls an individual to "wade in the water" or reminds them that "there is room in the kingdom," and the individual joins, rejects, or remains ambivalent to group song and worship.

"Climbing Jacob's Ladder," "Many Thousands Gone," and "Roll, Jordan, Roll" capture sacred religious visions. But that coded language was also used to indicate slaves escaping or other forms of disrupting masters' interest or spiritual consolation. More recently, poet and cultural critic Kevin Young claims that spirituals—whether entertainment, work song, or coded signal—fundamentally reveal the crucial imagining of actual freedom. Echoing scholars like C. Eric Lincoln, Lawrence Mamiya, and James Cone, Young explains that the performance of the song "transforms hope in the mere act of creating art out of slavery." Spirituals are not, Young insists, "just songs about everlasting but imminent disappearance."[24] Through the music, slaves who felt themselves inhuman could claim humanity; objects of history become agents in it; the purposeless space becomes a cosmos with purpose, capable of producing meaning, value, and overall significance for themselves and others. These historical, theological, social, and in some cases political dynamics constitute the occasion of the spirituals.

The major books on spirituals are forceful in their claims. Howard Thurman's *The Negro Spiritual Speaks of Life and Death* (1947), James Cone's *The Spirituals and the Blues* (1972), James Lovell's *Black Song* (1972), Sterling Stuckey's *Slave Culture* (1987), Joseph Brown's *To Stand on the Rock* (1998), and Kevin Young's *The Grey Album* (2012) all tackle questions such as whether the spirituals were merely parroted copies of whites' Protestant hymns or were complex theological folk tunes. Nearly every aspect of spirituals is debated. Does their content qualify as song or as folklore? Are they the basis of Black cultural tradition? If the spirituals are not born of whites, how much is from West Africa or how distinctive is the African influence? In the 1970s and 1980s, scholars were also preoccupied with questioning whether slaves accepted oppressive conditions, submitted to the slave master's will, or were capable of a revolutionary ethos ready to be mined for radical activities. What I want to point out is that in investigations of spirituals, from Du Bois's essays to Bernice Johnson Reagon's performances and writings to Young's poetic insights, the spirituals of enslaved Africans have been a key part of scholars and political thinkers demonstrating that indeed slaves had a culture of their own, a way of defining their own terms and politically resisting, a culture that was important to pass on to their children, one that nourished the wounds of racist social ills and energized political movements. I think that we can see far more in these songs through or outside the claims and oppositions previous scholars used to make sense of this powerfully generative Black music.

Seeing Saints

Thomas Higginson, Fredrika Bremer, Fanny Kemble, Frederick Law Olmsted, Frederick Douglass, and others witnessed the singing of spirituals and wrote about them detail in the mid-nineteenth century. Many white observers, for a variety of reasons, from overt racism and ethnocentric bias to ignorance, did not appreciate or encourage the singing and worshipping styles of enslaved Africans.[25] It is not uncommon to come across language that depicts the feelings of witnesses as escaping all words. These witnesses directly and indirectly point to counterlife in the spirituals through their attention to slaves' rapture, transcendence, and fervor while singing. It is here that singers and observers escape the utility of terms, knowledge, and understanding of this reality. The witnesses, moreover, wanted to get closer and penetrate further. In *Army Life in a Black Regiment* (1869), Thomas Higginson praised spirituals for their unbelievable power and wisdom, and he repeatedly tried to figure out how the ex-slaves composed the songs. Even after he discovered how spontaneous songs took root, whether they were improvised, dropped, or kept by the singers, he still remarked about how vague and distanced he felt from them. He wanted to use his writings, at least in part, to create a historical record of the singing itself, solidifying it as history in song. But the songs kept changing, the words were very hard to discern, and men in the regiment did not answer his questions. He reported the songs were part inviting and part mesmerizing, strikingly alienating for him even as a close observer.[26]

In *A Journey in the Seaboard Slave States* (1856), Frederick Law Olmsted was even more forthcoming about spirituals. While observing singing at a slave's funeral, after a sermon, Olmsted recounted that slaves engaged in "singing a *wild* kind of chant."[27] "An Old negro . . . raised a hymn which soon became a *confused chant*—the leader singing a few words alone, and then the company either repeating them or mak[ing] a response to them. . . . *I could understand but very few of the words.* The music was *wild and barbarous*."[28] Olmsted was convinced that he recognized Jesus in the religious expression, and he admired the informal demeanor, yet he also remained perplexed about the meaning behind all of it. The mending of bodies, the gesticulation, and the chants were beyond his comprehension. Many other reporters remarked on slaves' malleable use of words, moaning, shouting, and groaning. James L. Smith, a former slave, recounted how he and his fellow slaves worshipped in his *Autobiography*: "The way in which we worshipped is almost *indescribable*. The singing was accompanied by a certain *ecstasy of motion*, clapping of hands, tossing of heads, which *would continue without cessation* about half an hour, one would lead off a kind of recitative style, others joining in the chorus."[29] What Smith described, other writers, white and Black, referred to as the spirituals' "*wild* and *touching* pathos."[30]

Albert Raboteau describes the ring shout, one of the most recognizable forms of slaves singing spirituals. The shout would start with a leader calling out a verse of a spiritual while the shouters responded by walking around in circle. When the singers who stood outside the ring took the chorus, the shout proper would begin with the ring band shuffling rapidly to the beat announced by the handclapping and foot tapping of the chorus of singers who were said then to be "basing" the shouters.[31] I found a group of performers, the Singing and Praying Band from Delaware and Maryland, who were filmed at the Library of Congress, which I think gets closest to what the reporters describe: circular movement, shouting, moans, heightened consciousness through repetition, call-and-response.[32]

Like Smith, Douglass had a dual role as both witness and participant in singing. Douglass's remarks on slaves' singing in his 1845 *Narrative* give an individualized sociological view of the plantation. He explained that slaves permitted to go to "the Great House Farm" sang out: "I am going away to the Great House Farm."[33] This song is quite a literal recognition of what masters permitted the slave to do. The song is a declaration of who has the power over "I," where I am going when I pass away. The declaration of the "I" of the slave is an individual and communal commitment that defines one as a child of God, worthy of a seat in the Kingdom of Christ on earth and in heaven. It also serves other slaves, not converted, to tell them about the possible transformation that awaits them. Douglass is adamant about the philosophical depth of spirituals and the songs' impact on him; he explains that through the spirituals he first could articulate the dehumanizing character of slavery.[34] The songs reflect the enslaved Africans' "tale of woe."

Douglass was explicit about slaves' sorrow and philosophical depth to counter published sentiments expressing that proof of slaves' contentment with slavery was evidenced with their happy and simple singing. Harriet Jacobs's *Incidents in the Life of a Slave Girl* (1861) countered these claims as well. She wrote: "If you were to hear them at such times, you might think they were happy. But can that hour of *singing* and *shouting* sustain them through the dreary week, toiling without wages, under constant dread of the lash?"[35] Douglass and Jacobs both in different ways acknowledged and attributed sophistication and depth to the transformative point of view captured in the spirituals, but they were both emphatic that slaves' creative genius was no indication of happiness and still no acceptance of slavery.

What I find fascinating in Douglass especially is how he occupied multiple positions—participant and observer; defender and translator—but was seemingly sympathetic to what outsiders or strangers may have seen if they witnessed spirituals being sung. He continued to discuss the slaves on the way to the Great House Farm, writing:

> While on their way, they would make the dense old woods, for miles around, reverberate their *wild songs*, revealing *at once* the highest joy and the deepest sadness. They would compose and sing as they went along, consulting neither *time nor tune*. The thought that came up, came out—*if not in the word, in the sound*;—and as frequently in the one as in the other. They would sometimes sing the most pathetic sentiment in the most rapturous tone. . . . [T]hey would sing, as a chorus, to words which to many would seem unmeaning jargon, but which nevertheless, were full of meaning to themselves. . . . I did not, when a slave, understand the deep meaning of those rude and apparently incoherent songs . . . beyond my feeble comprehension; they were tones loud, long, and deep. . . . [H]earing of those wild notes always depressed my spirit.[36]

Douglass gives us a couple of lines referring to religious meaning, faith, latent rebellion, or allusions to freedom or heaven. This is the part that we know, that we can discern. We also know that shouts, movements, and moans create a mystical sense to bring heaven into the earthly material world. But when Douglass says "apparently incoherent songs" he implicitly critiques the language of other witnesses that denigrate the complexity, philosophical insight, and religious devotion of spiritual singing. He denies that songs are meaningless and incoherent, but he does not deny the rapturous, loud, deep, and moaning tones. While Douglass claims he did not understand fully the conceptual and theological depth of slave singing when he was a slave, how did he understand precisely what moans, groans, and shouts were from individuals in his company? Did the meaning of the songs need to be discerned, jargon-free, and coherent?

Feeling Frenzy

Decades later Du Bois wrote about the spirit-filled wild notes of slave singing and Black religious expression before emancipation. He also referred to the spirituals as uproarious, out of time and tune, and unceasing in their variety of expression. What others writers call rapturous sentiment, Du Bois called moments of "frenzy." He explained that the song and sermon culminate

> finally in the Frenzy or "Shouting"; when the spirit of the Lord passed by, and, seizing the devotee, made him mad with supernatural joy, was the last essential of Negro religion and the one more devoutly believed in than all the rest. It varied in expression from the silent rapt countenance or the low murmur and moan to the abandonment of physical fervor,—the stamping, shrieking, and shouting, the rushing to and fro and wild waving of arms, the weeping and laughing, the vision and the trance.[37]

Frenzy is a crucial staple that commentators, reporters, and scholars discuss. This part of the spirituals' aesthetic form is constituted by moans, shouts, and shrieks that communicate unknown meaning. What is the substance of the moans, the shouts, one's feeling of a connection to the divine? This is an epistemological problem that I do not answer, but I am conceptualizing what it is like to have something so crucial in its relation to the very form of the spiritual that is also something one cannot understand. Only the singer knows and feels their sense of knowing the way that they do; not even a fellow singer knows, and sometimes unaccountable unknowing is crucially sustained by all: witness and participants. Who knows specifically why someone chose to wade in water or why they wanted keys to the kingdom or when they received the spiritual validation, what they used it for beyond itself?

The spiritual sharing, felt along the trembling vibrato of the body, does not require in-depth psychoanalysis or priest's confessional—yet how can we record, stabilize, or make our intellectual object that which is irreverent to recording, discernment, or stability? The spirituals, then, contain an affirming contradiction: on the one hand, they are a bold confirmation of singing the community and self into biblical myth, social history, and religious transformation; on the other hand, the specifics—what is communicated—consist of beautiful and powerful sounds from listeners and participants that one cannot fully make out. One could argue that one does not need to know exactly what a groan means, and it is precisely the expression of where words fail and every important beat and sound take over. But my point is that there is a story there; there is a form of narrative, a reason for the calls and wonderful wild notes of response, yet its power relies on it, songs' inarticulate rapture along with what cannot be known or what can be discerned only partially. The spiritual form emphasizes clear historical, political, mythical valence, but this clarity is overwhelmed by improvising and spontaneous difference; it produces individuals, groups, and the relations among both. The individuals can express or withhold as much as they want of their transformative story and still fulfill the group; the group straddles the greater narrative and individual words and sounds.

Hurston famously wrote about spirituals after emancipation, but her words are pertinent for slave singing as well. Hurston distinguished between songs that were the outgrowth of Fisk University glee clubs and "genuine spirituals."[38] "Neo-spirituals," as she called them, were beautiful, but she did not categorize them as spirituals for one major reason: spirituals rely on "jagged harmony," "dissonances," and key changes.[39] Hurston emphasizes, "The congregation is bound by no rules." Hurston leads us to believe it is radical difference itself that points to the singing of each song as a new creation—the singing of a song is never a final thing but a "mood." The songs will never be sung the same way twice. They don't stay in the same form for long. The "mood" that the singers express is repeatedly refined by the group to fit the form. One anonymous slave recalled that the group works to express the mood as "dey work it in you know; till dey get it right; and dat's de way."[40] The working it in, as Hurston interprets it, stems from the *"expression of feeling"*—to the point where consciousness is lost—where individuals and the group achieve limitless space in the new and original arrangement.[41]

Even after Hurston and others break down the form and substance of spirituals as much as they can, one cannot make sense of the specifics of what one undergoes in a loss of consciousness, which is defined by a loss of words and overall coherency. Bringing heaven down to earth relies on this experience. There is intellectual powerlessness in assessing the gravity of the spirituals' great force.

How can subject/object relations, designed on coherency of position, what one knows of someone else, and whose interests the object serves, sustain themselves when the forms of knowledge we recognize fundamentally unravel? The attempt to answer or work through this question is why I submit that we read spirituals through the thingness of persons—as performative episodes where conventional subject/object relations break down. This is not my effort to refer to enslaved Africans as things but to realize more fully how singing Africans express the thingness of persons to which we all have access. Spirituals, when performed, express a marvelous sense of contradiction that need not be reconciled, but such performance forces or asks us to think more seriously about how people embody and express mutually conflicting modes of communication—the indelible fact of partial knowing and unknowing from the perspective of participant, witness, and critic.

"Every man trying to express himself through song. Every man for himself," Hurston proclaims.[42] But shouts, moans, and verses, between audiences and groups or among the group itself, can't detail or express specificity, what that individual expresses about one's transformation or about God's salvation, about gratitude, about the worthiness of failed or renewed moral commitments, and about a master's mistreatment and hypocrisy. I want to think about the thingness of persons in spirituals to grapple with contradictory and irreverent force in spirituals. Fredrika Bremer made a profound statement about spirituals when she said the improvisational, spontaneous, and radical transformational aspects of the spiritual reflected everyday social life that was also filled with unaccountable disruptions.[43] Thus, unaccountable thingness in spirituals also reflects what is disruptive and unwieldy about social life. The spirituals can help us expand and deepen the question we ask about enslaved Africans and how they sought to make sense of the institutional pressures they faced by establishing their own sense of value, meaning, and purpose—and more specifically how they did so in excess of our contemporary interests in the politics of freedom.

In one of Aretha Franklin's famous renditions of "Precious Lord (Part 2)," she describes the speaker as being "at the river."[44] The river is a metaphor for a number of religious moments, among them a crossing from sin to God's salvation. Another version of this spiritual discovery and renewal of crossing over can be found in the song "Wade in the Water." After emphasizing that trouble, not peace, is the crux of the song—"God's gonna trouble the water"—Joseph Brown explains: "Imagine how that song is constructed. Whoever is singing is an elder. Children, wade in the water. Whoever is singing it is on the other side. Saying, come on now, you can do this, come on now, you can do this. . . . As soon as you get out there [*in the water*] it's gonna make you feel like you're gonna drown, you're gonna panic, you gonna be scared, you gonna flail. So why don't you hold on each other's hands, because your life is demanding that you get into trouble, not avoid it."[45] The location of the river is where the community ignites with jubilation and identification. It is the location of stillness, contemplation, and most of all humility and vulnerability. For the shouters and singer the past and present blur. I am or I was, too, at the river. Why? Why was I pleading for a merciful and benevolent God to take my hand? The community shouts, cries, wails, and weeps in trepidation, courage, and triumph. In each shout is their unity and diversity, the universal and particular. How did they arrive there? What trouble *do* they face? One has the courage to confront, but what is the story of trouble, and what form does it take? The answers to these questions may or may not be answered and need not be. But the problem, the change, and the transformation are there to mirror, elaborate, and change one's relationship to self, to other, to God. The form and the song tell the story, and they hide a multitude of stories that are, are yet to come, and have passed.

The collective structure of story, ritual, and participation forms a community, but this unity is inherently divided by the specifics of each person's own story and how they got to the water. It is unknown to the other members or audience, and even if someone knows something about another's experience, the expression, combination, and rendition are made new so that even the known is remade as unknown as it is performed.

Johnson also captures what historians, folklorists, theologians, musicologists, and others interested in spirituals know: the singers of the first American art form were Black, brilliant, and provocative, and they constructed songs with a sense of immediate and biblical history and myth, layered symbolism, and the spontaneity of John Coltrane and Walt Whitman. The spirituals are expressions of the group, but they harbor what Johnson says is unique to the blues or what makes the blues different from spirituals. About the blues, Johnson writes, "They are the philosophical expression of the individual contemplating his situation in relation to the conditions surrounding him."[46] Each spiritual contains the unknown facet of the individual even as it expresses the exhortation of the group. It brings a different meaning to Johnson's use of *unknown* in his poem titled "O Black and Unknown Bards." The story of how someone is called to wade in the water is not fully known. Thus, a significant aspect of spirituals, from a critical perspective, provokes and necessitates a more explanatory burden that powerfully escapes explanation.

For example, at the end of Baldwin's *Go Tell It on the Mountain* (1950) John Grimes sees his journey to salvation through the song "If It Cost Me My Life."[47] If we heard the song without knowing John's life we would fill in the details with our own or someone else's, and this points to the welcome negativity of spirituals' abstraction. To look for counterlife in spiritual performance is to observe lives in what is withheld, expressed, and inexpressible in the wading in the water, the crossing over Jordan, or the climbing of Jacob's ladder.

Lord, Hear My Cry

Performer and scholar Bernice Johnson Reagon says that in and through moans, groans, and shouts a fundamental transformation takes place through singing spirituals. "The song is how we run sound through our body. *The sound changes us.*"[48] When she sings "Precious Lord (Part 2)," Aretha Franklin says, "ain't no harm to moan." When she moans and hums she exemplifies transformation, and I take great interest not only in Aretha but in shouts and flights that invigorate and exult in the performance. She utters the profound simplicity of the song words—stretching them with voices, commanding them with enigmatic passion and an energetic flurry of piano keys; the community merges with her through its exhortations— identifications and witnessing that affirm communal experience with infinite variation. Each person is struck with enough clarity of vision and conviction, yet every person's vision, thoughts, cries remain only partially articulated by standing at the river, the crossroads, the water that awaits God's troubling.

There is a clip of Aretha Franklin singing one of her great gospel songs, "Precious Memories," at the White House, where she experiences a moment of spiritual power and excess as a physical ailment likely attributable to her overall health and age.[49] The Williams Brothers, who accompany her, testify: "Somebody got to know there's church up in here tonight." The room was blown away by the performance of Franklin and the Williams Brothers. Franklin comments, "I heard my grandmother say, many years ago when I was just a child, . . . [s]he would moan around the house." "He'll be God in every hour" is what she says. Unlike in the song performance of "Precious Lord (Part 2)," Aretha begins to tell stories about other gospel singers like Shirley Caesar. She reflects on the past that substantiates the current moment. As LeRhonda S. Manigault-Bryant offers, "Music operates as a performative feature of lived memory."[50] But the exhausted Aretha's lived memory gives us only fragments that cannot be pieced together as something whole.

From a distance, it is no doubt that Franklin's presence and performance in the White House can be discussed in terms of the failure or success of racial progress, the moment's radical potential, or neoliberal acceptance or celebration of the status quo. This version of critique admittedly came to me first. Yet, I also wondered what Franklin's moaning calls our attention to. As Franklin was humming along I could not help but think about my own mother, grandmother, and aunts and the humming and moaning around my house and the random quotes of biblical verse that came to me as a child hanging out in places where I wasn't supposed to be. What I find miraculous about the Franklin moment here and her other performances of songs like "Precious Lord (Part 2)" is how the flash of Franklin's grandmother, her ancestor, whom I don't know, gave me a clear window into my own senses and memory of the history of guidance from loved ones. My grandma used to mouth the words to the Impressions' song—"That's right," she'd say; "you got to 'Keep on Pushing.' . . . Don't let anyone or anything hold you back."

Admittedly these words sat with me, but the depth of clarity of Aretha's moans is not more apparent. The specific story is still lost. Yet, I cannot watch and listen to this without being moved by her spiritual declarations and musical exuberance. And perhaps, Franklin's moan, the site of her grandmother's wisdom without a proverb, defines the transformational power of sound that magnifies the spirituals. The counterlife in Aretha's performance tells us that we can be historical without historical precision, that we can have philosophical depth without the epigram, and that we can mine irreconcilable contradiction without concrete political fulfill-ment—we often don't know what is in someone's head despite the institu-tional and objectifying powers they face. Perhaps it is that balance between spiritual affirmation and the longing for expression and knowledge of it that draws us to the song: to say, as Douglass did, when remembering the ring shout, "I was myself within the circle."[51]

4

THE LAST BLACK HERO

I stood there with the trains plunging in and out, throwing blue sparks. What did they ever think of us transitory ones? Ones such as I had been before I found Brotherhood—birds of passage who were too obscure for learned classification, too salient for the most sensitive recorders of sound; of natures too ambiguous for the most ambiguous words, and too distant from the centers of historical decision to sign or even to applaud the signers of historical documents? We who write no novels, histories or other books. What about us, I thought . . .
—Ralph Ellison, *Invisible Man*

In the last chapter I claimed that the thingness in persons as a kind of counterlife is an important way to approach the singing performances of enslaved Africans. Thingness is the remainder one can find after realizing that subject/object distinctions do not fully capture the layered assemblages that spirituals exemplify. Another way of understanding comes from the notion that when slaves sang themselves into biblical stories, as God's children, they reclaimed a moral practice from oppressive slave owners rooted in the slaves' total exclusion from God's kingdom, obsequious relationships to their masters, and thoughts of unredeemable immorality. Thus, the spirituals' reinvention of culture, self, other, and group through song forms a counternarrative. It is not far-fetched to say that the first American art form, the spiritual, is also a form of counternarrative and counterhistory. But does counterhistory have a counterlife?

Counterhistory, from a variety of vantage points (those of scholars, politicians, artists), is crucial to Black cultural traditions in the United States and throughout Black diasporas. Like reinventions of Moses, Toussaint Louverture, or Harriet Tubman, counterhistories can focus on heroes, but what happens to other figures of the community who impact the actions of the heroic protagonists? Are they forgotten remainders, or do they become figures of the next counterhistory? Added up, this means that counterhistory is never singular; counterhistory, accidently, inevitably, or by design, cannot be an end to itself. A function of counterhistory, then, is to produce more counterhistories as part of an ongoing engagement with transformative possibility in marginalized and oppressed communities. In this chapter I explore how the function of counterhistory produces and reveals a sustained entanglement with counterhistory/history, truth/falsehood, certainty/uncertainty, and normative/radical that I read as counterhistory's counterlife.

Is all Black history counterhistory? It seems that because Black people have been subjugated for centuries and whites have controlled the narrative of this reality, one could readily answer yes. One could think of all Black history as dismantling the master's house with the master's tools, correcting the official story that indirectly or directly reinforces racist systems of oppression and inequality.[1] Surely the significance of counterhistory is not about mastering truth but telling a story with the sources of the oppressors that will inspire political consciousness and action. About scholars' interest in and use of slavery, Stephen Best contends that the slave past is considered a "vital dimension of the effort to define Black political goals."[2] Walter Benjamin encouraged us to comb sources against the grain in an effort to liberate archives for political and intellectual advantage: to give voices to victims with the tools of the victors.[3] Saidiya Hartman claims that such counterhistorical projects have failed because such histories slip in the grounds of necessary traction—remaining disruptive and insurgent—but nonetheless remain permanent outliers.[4] Best and Hartman, while they may see counternarrative and counterhistory differently, agree that to an overwhelming degree slavery studies seeks the uses of history to impact various modes of being political in the present. Walter Benn Michaels protests the stakes of history altogether when it comes to creating political equality in the present. "My point," advances Michaels, "is only that the interest in the past shouldn't be mistaken for an analysis of or an attempt to deal with problems of the present."[5] Michaels's claims strongly suggest that while the history of Black suffering and overcoming is significant for historical reasons, it is not necessary to produce reverential or revolutionary counterhistories rooted in Blackness to transform present inequality.

The counterlife of counterhistory, in this sense, is to think about counterhistory as an object that can be valued outside of its immediate political uses. But still, it is through the possibility of its political use as an affective force that we initially understand counterhistory's potential. One of the ways counterhistory seduces readers and observers is by the absence of or the longing to see or read about particular figures, especially Black male heroes. One thing one hears casually, from mentors at the Boys and Girls Clubs to icons like President Barack Obama, from community activists to scholars thinking about concepts of Black progress: "we need more heroes." In 1843, when Henry Highland Garnet tried to inspire the insurrection of slaves, he drew on "the heroes of the American Revolution."[6] Garnet exclaimed: "Patient sufferers! . . . [L]et it no longer be a debatable question whether it is better to choose Liberty or death."[7]

This heroic occasion can take many forms, from giants like President Obama to other heroes who somehow capture the heroic morally and politically. Nate Parker wanted to tell Nat Turner's story in order to tell a story about Black heroes because heroes in art help us "to face injustice."[8] Referring to individuals like Nat Turner or Harriet Tubman, Ellison repeated in his essays that Black people and culture were heroic for fashioning a way of life through violence and adversity. Looking at iconic people in this history can inspire others to struggle for various visions of Black communal liberation.[9] Part of this idea is for someone to act on the front lines to combat racist stereotypes and characterizations that support or lead to oppressive policies and white supremacist thinking generally. Most of these heroes are Black men that sacrifice themselves for Black community, democratic and Christian ethics, and the idyllic promise of America.

I examine three slave texts in this chapter that I read as counterhistories. These texts feature romantic Black masculine heroes who take on or gesture to official forms, types, and genres of accepted knowledge, then depart from them through subversive critiques. These texts are all fictional, but they are dynamic in making or signaling interventions in real-world political thinking and activity. The first is the story of Madison Washington, whom Garnet identifies as "the bright star of freedom."[10] As part of his openness to violence as a means of freedom for slaves, Douglass composed the Madison Washington story in a historical novella. Douglass recalled the American revolutionary hero as an accepted and established script to reinvent through his storytelling. Douglass was prompted by his sense that US history's halls of revolution have no slave hero. Slave heroes were necessary and important to abolitionists' political uses of history. I also turn to the "Catcher Freeman" (2008) episode of Aaron McGruder's *Boondocks* television cartoon. "The Story of Catcher Freeman" portrays the very demand and significance of a Black history. It is a counterhistory of counterhistories. The last counterhistory is a cowboy film crossed with a slave narrative, Quentin Tarantino's *Django Unchained* (2012). Tarantino radicalizes the western by putting slavery at the center, but he also radicalizes the Black hero in such way that it is not clear whether the protagonist Django is either heroic or Black. What is more, this male-centered slave story reflexively prompts us to ask about the important role of minor figures (other slaves or seemingly minor female characters) in calls for or silencing of new counterhistories.

I am interested in how these heroic counterhistories seek to become well-known history, and in this process of legitimacy and proliferation, counterhistories reveal more subjugated figures, events, and knowledges, which in turn become fodder for more counterhistories that could be explored and recovered. In this process, truth—what really happened, who the real hero is, the focus of the story, and what constitutes a Black slave hero—gets thrown into question repeatedly and is never answered. This unresolvable instability defines the counterlife of counterhistory. Studying these texts of enslaved Africans reveals how counterhistory is ongoing in both its reaffirmation and its unsettling of meaning, truth, and believable history. This, I advance, is how the counterlife of enslaved Africans and the very notion of counterhistory remain mutually imbricated.

Unheroic Slaves

Patrick Henry and Thomas Jefferson are heroes for different reasons, the former of the Revolutionary War and the other of the Declaration of Independence and US political leadership. Virginia claims these valiant figures. These historical icons beg the question of Douglass's *Heroic Slave*'s premise: is there any Black person that embodies Christianity, enlightenment, and the violent heart of a lion in Virginia's slave population, and can hidden or unknown archives reveal such a person? If so, making this story available could combat the historical absence of Africans striving for enlightened perfection, masculine sovereignty, and political inclusion.

Douglass's hero, Madison, is as equally an idyllic figure as Henry and Jefferson. Madison is saintly, heroic, and a lover of freedom in its transcendental and practical possibility. Douglass's story of Madison is based on a real person from Virginia's history, and Douglass's ultimate goal is to use the novel form to enshrine this person in history and galvanize this history as part of the larger shouting demand for action, financial support, and overall favor for the abolitionist movement. The generative political power of the book relies on its acceptance and interrogation from wider circles of readers (or at least serving as fresh material for apathetic sympathizers). The novella then generates official lore for the annals of the state, yet stimulates the radical energies of countermovements. This dual imperative is as much necessary as it is simultaneous and contradictory.

More important, the action within the story of Madison's triumph over his captors leads one to believe in finality or completion in his victory, yet within this finality the novella sustains and encourages more forgotten histories and subjugated knowledges that may or not become part of the state record of heroes or radical politics. Nonetheless, these forgotten histories and subjugated knowledges come to light to reveal what often goes unrealized about social conflict.

Early in *The Heroic Slave*, Madison asks, what "is life to me?"[11] This question has no certain answers beyond his compelling desire to seek freedom, but is desiring freedom all there is in Madison's predicament? Madison has a wife and children. While he loves his wife, he feels driven toward freedom and ultimately leaves her in hopes of being free. What are the values and social attachments that make Madison want to go back for his wife but that do not directly correspond to how whites impact daily lives? The novella narrates a story of heroic triumph, but what is equally important is how the story discloses a subtext of slaves' unpredictability and enigmatic thinking that exceeds Madison's thirst for freedom. In fact, it is really this sense of enigma that helps us to see the unheroic aspects of the novella, where remainders of the counterhistory lie. Madison's wife, plantation slaves, and Madison's coconspirators aboard the slave ship are characters that cannot be named or can't be made into heroes or counterhistories that history calls attention to because they make the hero possible. These minor figures provoke enigmas and a problem for the protagonist hero about the possibilities and alternatives that the text does not account for. Heroism, bravery, and the failure of such texts are in Madison to the degree that the minor acts of others become discourse on unheroic everyday life instead of new heroism meant to inspire collective projects.

Madison is a slave like others, but what prompted him into becoming someone who cannot stand to be in shackles? Madison's masters flog him for staying at the mill too long. This disciplining stands as a punishment and warning, a way to police and dominate Madison's behavior and that of other slaves, yet paradoxically, the flogging is actually a motivating factor in Madison's escape. Still, after he escapes, he risks being recaptured because he wants to free his wife and children, whom he cannot stop thinking about.[12] While one could reduce this to an attachment to slavery itself or an ideology of love, such a reduction diminishes and oversimplifies human thought and the interpersonal connection that Douglass conveys. What actually inspires Madison's moves is unclear, but that shouldn't stop readers from asking what the probable factors are for his actions. There is no way to obscure, blot out, or eradicate a slave's unpredictability—the brutal fact is that however much one whips, sexually assaults, overworks, or rewards a person, one can never know what is going on in that person's head. For anyone who desires to impose their will or interests on a community of actors, this epistemological problem is a fundamentally social one too, as it shapes how people relate to themselves and others.[13]

There can be no greater example of this than in the retelling of the circumstances of the insurrection led by Madison. After Madison escapes from slavery initially, he is recaptured and ends up aboard the *Creole*, where he leads an insurrection. Madison's revolt has already happened in the novella when Douglass introduces the reader to some sailors at a coffeehouse in Richmond who are discussing it. One sailor, Jack Williams, argues the insurrection could have been prevented or safely contained. Williams is confident that every Negro slave is a coward simply because the slave is Black. With six resolute white men, Williams says, he could have the Blacks in chains in ten minutes.[14] The boastful and confident Williams turns to the practice that was supposed to subdue Madison when he stayed at the mill too long—"flogging"—but flogging may not be enough, and Williams goes on to explain that he would use other means of violence to "quell a nigger insurrection."[15]

But this is where Williams tries to have it both ways. He claims that slaves are cowards and that cowardice is their nature, but if slaves are fundamentally cowards, what is the origin of the experiential knowledge on how to quell insurrections? If all one needed was to crack a whip, there would be no such thing as "rebellious darkies," and the thought of rebellion would not even occur to a Sambo interested in furthering his master's interests.[16] Williams's misrecognition of what motivates slaves begs the question, what *does* motivate slaves?

Douglass's novella, moreover, wants to claim that slaves, if given the opportunity, can be heroic, but my point is to show that what a slave is thinking about cannot be certain, and even though the character may be thinking about rebelling, he could be unwilling to actualize the rebellion for reasons other than cowardice or the master's absolute dominion. The culture of domination has built into itself that slaves are capable of insurrection for a variety of unknown reasons. The conditions of possibility have instability baked into the cake, even while the sailor Williams insists that white supremacy always maintains the upper hand through knowledge and violence, chalking the revolt up to white incompetence. Walter Johnson's study of the *Creole*, however, unveils that slaves aboard the ship with different personal and political interests (which the novella withholds) temporarily aligned with one another and decided to rebel.[17]

Douglass emphasized the ongoing sense of instability and contingency with which I identify. The most eloquent moment in the book occurs when Douglass attributes Madison's and his fellow slaves' courage to the sea. Douglass writes about the sea's spiritual encouragement: "lonely billows of the Atlantic . . . every breeze speaks of courage and liberty."[18] The sailor Williams is skeptical, claiming that, whether at sea or on land, the slave is a coward. What the sea communicates is the notion that something— a change of conditions perhaps, together with inspiration (via Madison)— can change the lot of slaves. Douglass's text revolves around the possibilities of radical and unexpected change. The sea exemplifies this effect and reality. Agents, actors, and new information mean that a compressed state that defines Negro character is unreliable, and self-risk and what slaves take risks for might be prompted by the desire for freedom or for something else he or she finds valuable.

Does this change how we see Madison's wife or the other slaves who, unlike Madison, are not interested in revolting or escaping? While Douglass implies the sea is crucial in conveying the ethos of freedom, the unpredictability in human subjects—that the sea makes manifest—points us back to when Madison tries to avoid slaves from his plantation. He believes if they discover him they will betray him. While the "negroes [on the *Creole*] fairly worshipped him," his fellow plantation slaves were less poised and were flat-out uninterested in freedom.[19] They certainly didn't worship him. What did the slaves think about Madison? What did they think about their fellow slaves or the idea of escape? Douglass does not go to great lengths to explain the difference between the ship slaves and the slaves on the plantation; he only says the ship slaves worshipped Madison and that the plantations slaves would betray him if they knew that he was plotting escape. But why aren't these slaves on the ship the same as the ones Madison encounters on his own plantation? Douglass writes: "Peeping through the rents of the quarters, I saw my fellow slaves seated by a warm fire, merrily passing away the time, as though their hearts knew no sorrow. Although I envied their seeming contentment, all the wretched as I was, I despised the cowardly acquiescence in their own degradation which it implied. . . . I dared not enter the quarter—, for where there is seeming contentment with slavery, there is certain treachery to freedom."[20] Masters and/or slaves have deceived themselves into "contentment with slavery." But why don't the slaves aboard the *Creole* turn Madison in? Is it the sea or some new conditions that shape slaves' proclivity to act? Madison may be wrong about the degree to which slaves have acquiesced; he may also be wrong about his own predisposition to change their minds. Madison and the sailor Williams misdiagnose slaves' interiority or at least fail to admit that they do not know why or how long slaves will cowardly acquiesce. If Madison believed his fellow slaves were all cowards, then he would have never attempted a revolt, and if the white sailors believed slaves were all capable of rebellion, then they would not have been blindsided.

Douglass's *Heroic Slave* imbues the text with unpredictability and error. The novella shows that even slavery's fiercest scenes of domination contain proliferations of the wildest contingencies, which need to be further explored as part of slavery's archive. One of the most overlooked mysteries in *The Heroic Slave* is why Madison chose to leave his wife and children in the first place. When Madison tries to rescue his wife, she is shot dead. When Madison says, "I shall be free," he commits himself to the likelihood that he will never see his wife again. Are we to believe him when he says their "parting was like flesh from bones"?[21] He chooses for five years to leave his wife and live in a cave near his master's plantation, but it isn't a heroic burst of courage that drives him toward freedom; it is a great fire.[22] Otherwise, Madison stays in hiding. He says, "I had partly become content with my mode of life."[23] Madison's love for his wife is paradoxical. It sustains him from "utter despair," yet this sustenance encourages his ambition to be free; it is because of this forceful attachment that he does not want to leave her.[24]

During the five years of bringing him provisions, how did Madison's wife procure his food and keep his whereabouts secret from malicious parties? Along with caring for their children, I wonder what values and practices sustained her connection to Madison. The context of the relationship is the potential for escape and the refusal of it; the five years is a stalemate in historical progress, yet rife in the possibilities of historical thinking. Madison's and his wife's survival during this interim period is not heroic, yet the circumstances make for an interesting vehicle into the social life that is estranged from the monuments of political history and point to a gap in understanding that needs to be hypothesized, rendered, and expressed. This social life is full of moral probing, ethical choices, and agonizing feelings of despair and hope that might be legitimate on their own historical grounds. As much as *The Heroic Slave* establishes an example of masculine agential violence, it also cues us to turn our attention away from our own political impulses—to look for agency, resistance, or the elasticity of power. Douglass provides us with an opportunity to explore counterlife and reaffirm that slavery contains both the discernible and ungraspable aspects of everyday life. This would mean taking on the subject matter of the nameless slaves, the rebels and harbors of Madison's secret, and Madison's nameless wife. The nameless here are the unheroic or unmythical figures that make Madison Washington's narrative possible. Slaves enabled Madison or looked the other way. Scholars of slavery have given us pictures of slaves' investment in freedom, citizenship, personhood, and womanhood, but Madison and his wife's five-year life point us to multiple sets of overlapping circumstances that include other workers and slaves and their practices (preparing/consuming goods) who may have different immediate interests and motivations on the plantation.[25]

Would accounts of these people and practices count as counterhistory to be revered and remembered and owned and disseminated? Slaves took or gave food and knowledge in exchange for other objects of interest and value, which enabled, blocked, or had nothing to do with Madison's escape. These are all efforts of slaves to transform their lives within the circulation of knowledge and goods on the plantation. These efforts are significant to conceptualizing slave social life and yet could be related only tangentially to slave freedom or disruptions to white power. To reimagine this kind of work, these practices, and such exchange is fodder for counterhistory, though not in a traditional sense, but rather it radicalizes the historical lens by expanding it to value equally the unheroic family memory, storytelling, and folk myth alongside heroic tales that have the most political visibility.

"Catcher Freeman"

Douglass wanted Madison's story to be told and retold, printed and reprinted, accepted as history. If Madison remained a folktale passed down from generation to generation, we have the situation of "The Story of Catcher Freeman" episode from Aaron McGruder's *Boondocks*. The "Catcher Freeman" episode features a mythical slave hero named Catcher Freeman who, according to the cartoon, is little known to history and whose actual existence seems debatable. In this episode, the story of Catcher Freeman gets retold from a variety of perspectives, and even though he is a Black freedom fighter it is unclear what each storyteller's motivations are for telling the story beyond having the legitimacy of their voice recognized and accepted by the group. Neither the abolition of slavery nor civil rights legislation nor shouts of Black Lives Matter is at stake with this cartoon satire of a heroic slave. However, McGruder calls on us to rethink and reexamine the truth, value, and relevance of a counterhistory of heroic enslaved Africans for our contemporary moment.

McGruder's *Boondocks* cartoons graced American newspapers from 1996 to 2006. McGruder transformed the popularity of these dark comedic vignettes by turning them into a television cartoon series, which started in 2005 and lasted for four seasons; the fourth and final season ended in 2014. McGruder was not involved with the final season. The major characters are Robert (Granddad) Freeman, Huey Freeman, Riley Freeman, Uncle Ruckus, Tom, and Jazmine. Robert claims to be a hero, but he turns out to be a genuine, caring opportunist interested in the little he did for civil rights as an opportunity to claim that he has been robbed of his rightful place and purpose in history—next to Martin L. King, Rosa Parks, and Jesse Jackson. Huey is a Black Nationalist living in the suburbs. Riley, Huey's little brother, is a childish incarnation of street culture fantasy and an ongoing indictment of how infantile stereotypical street culture is. Tom, the neighbor, is married to a white woman named Sarah. Tom and Sarah have a mixed-race child named Jazmine who has a crush on Huey. Perhaps the most infamous is Uncle Ruckus. He turns up everywhere at every job in every time period as a Black person who is the most flamboyant racist, including against himself, yet his only friends who tolerate him are not like-minded whites (obviously) but the Freeman family.

The "Catcher Freeman" episode aired in January 2008. The episode centers on the legend of a Freeman ancestor who led slaves to escape. We are given the impression that there is one major important story that is hidden from schoolbooks and institutionalized curriculum. Robert "Granddad" Freeman inherited the story and was brought in as a special witness to this valuable and heroic truth. But by the episode's end Huey, Granddad, Uncle Ruckus, and Riley all have their own ways of telling the story. "Catcher Freeman" brings the romantic Black historical mode into everyday life and showcases a story of the depersonalizing treatment of slaves, which communicates how the personality of the storyteller shapes the genre and content of the story. Yet at the same time, the everyday voices gathered around the living room of the Freeman household use myth to express personal interest and perspective. The notion that "Catcher Freeman" is significant for the Black collective shifts from the credible and useful to the ridiculous; emphasizing the heroic collective importance of the story becomes an opportunity for self-aggrandizement and validation of the storyteller's worldview. The role of truth cannot be distinguished from the idea that "this is my truth." There is an implicit agreement that the performance of "my truth" supersedes an authentic occasion to exchange newly accepted facts. In episodes of *The Boondocks* this scripting is rigorous to the degree that all that really matters to the storytellers is that the stories are theirs.

Overall, McGruder's *Boondocks* is no stranger to a revisionist and counterfactual history of American heroes. The premise for one episode was that Martin Luther King was not dead, was in a coma, and then reemerged in a new movement. The movement then failed and ended with King telling a crowd of political pushers and partygoers that they were a bunch of niggers. *The Boondocks* worked through a sarcastic and unconventional take on history. McGruder's cartoons are funny and manage to offend just about everyone in some way, but he also establishes vital truth, and the episodes tend to deliver a kernel of truth through sledgehammers of unexpected insight.[26]

When slavery is discussed in *The Boondocks*, McGruder focuses the narrative on someone whom people know little about, like Madison Washington. While Douglass's Madison Washington is less known but real, Catcher Freeman is unknown and a total fiction. The idea still in both accounts is not to bring out different heroes but to return to the foundational idea that a slave can be a hero. It is important for Granddad that Huey and

Riley know that Catcher Freeman is their blood ancestor. But Granddad is known to his grandchildren for exaggerating the family's impact on history. When Granddad begins the story, Riley and Huey assume a skeptical disposition they're quite familiar with. The Black hero appears from Granddad's eternal powers of recollection and Riley says: "Granddad, you always telling about someone related to us," like Jackie Robinson. An unknown Black hero, instead of a white hero, is something that McGruder anticipates as his joke.

In "Catcher Freeman" we get three, almost four, different takes on Catcher Freeman's history: Granddad's, Uncle Ruckus's, Huey's, and Riley's. Huey consults the Internet, and Riley doesn't tell his Catcher Freeman story but indicates the radical changes he would make to the story if he'd been given a chance to tell his version. All these takes on Catcher Freeman work as counterhistories, moving an unknown figure to a known one with each story countering the others with evidence, sources, ideology, and perspective.

Granddad's Catcher Freeman story is an unapologetic romance. Granddad insists that Catcher Freeman was not only great but he was a relative. This could be yet another instance of his exaggerating past heroism, not just promoting himself but exulting the family lineage. Riley sees Granddad insisting on possibly being related to Catcher Freeman as the first sign of a lie and insists that Granddad is always trying to connect the family to someone famous. "That nigga lyin," says Riley.[27] Riley has no faith in Granddad's latest rendition of heroic family glory and is skeptical of Granddad's convenient history of another heroic Black relative. "I told you Catcher Freeman is not only your ancestor, but he is real," proclaims Granddad. Granddad Freeman proudly claims that Catcher Freeman was the greatest Black man who ever lived. He was Malcolm X, Nat Turner, and Barack Obama rolled into one.

Granddad insists on telling the story. He begins it as a myth among slaves. Slaves hear rumors that Catcher is coming to help free them. Riley interrupts throughout the story, pointing out that Granddad's attempts to jazz up the story for credibility do not work. Granddad's version of history has the Black hero and his heroine, Thelma (Catcher's wife in Granddad's version), side by side in a romantic picture. And that's exactly how it happened; it's the truth. Granddad, the self-proclaimed civil rights veteran, is routinely caught flat-out lying about history to serve his own self-aggrandizement or self-interest. Even so, he does so in the name of broader Black people's or families' interests, and if Granddad does something great, it is usually by accident and reframed as courage, bravery, and sacrifice for Black people. "Exactly truth," in Granddad's case, can be precisely false, and telling a story that can somehow benefit a Black group can really be rooted in selfish motivations. Granddad's version of Catcher Freeman is a counter-romance that shows a Black hero against all odds who marries a light-skinned heroine. McGruder ironizes the Black heroic romance by actually casting it in such explicitly romantic terms that Granddad's credibility cannot endure Riley's sense of disbelief. Riley repeatedly interrupts Granddad, expressing skepticism at just about every point where Granddad proclaims an undeniable fact. Granddad's rendition never achieves the historical confirmation he wants other than the insistence on his fantasy and what the force of believing it can do for Riley and Huey as Black youth in need of a heroic past.

Uncle Ruckus is a Black person who is quite proud of hating Black people. He walks in just after Granddad finishes his Catcher story. He overhears the end of the story and begins to tell his own version. Ruckus begins with an offensive, ludicrous, yet hilarious introduction: "Back in slavery, when the world made sense. . . ." Riley does not believe any of Granddad's story, but when Ruckus portrays Catcher as a slave catcher, who resembles a beast obsessed with catching slaves, Riley is intrigued. Ruckus's story comes right from white racist characterizations of Blacks as beasts, but Catcher's beastliness is "good" because he serves the interests of whites. Riley, doubting Granddad, believes every single word of Ruckus's titillating story of Freeman hiding underwater and in trees, catching runaway slaves.

Ruckus explains the need for Catcher by explaining slavery as a big party. White masters threatened slaves with "time-outs" when the slaves rebelled or misbehaved. Ruckus always toes the racist line of the established rhetoric of conservative Southern historians of the Dunning school that treats the Confederacy sympathetically. Ruckus repeatedly emphasizes that Blacks want more freedom and leisure than they deserve. What I find most interesting is that Ruckus finds community with his Black friends by telling his story, even though the story reflects his racist worldview. Ruckus suggests that his truth should be retold. He doubles down on the significance of the past, the forces of ideological rhetoric, and the heroic Black person, yet solely through the viewpoint of white supremacy. Riley loves it, a stinging indictment of the childishness, naivete, and simplicity of youth, gangster culture on TV, and the reduction of Black life and death.

Ruckus and Granddad don't effectively care about anything but being believed by the children in the room. It's a battle between them; it's a battle for the youth who are glaring at both with sustained incredulity. Huey, the resident radical, wants to settle the dispute between Ruckus and Granddad by researching Catcher on the Internet. "We can resolve this," Huey says. The story online is different in key ways. Thelma was looking for freedom. Thelma leads a revolt, and the story that was about a heroic man actually becomes a narrative about a heroic and courageous woman. Catcher, in Huey's story, is actually Tobias, the sellout from Granddad's story. Thelma ends up the hero of the less-predictable narrative, and in trying to shoot Thelma, Catcher shoots the master instead and inadvertently becomes a hero. And then Catcher (Tobias) goes with the winning team out of convenience, and the legend is born. Neither Ruckus nor Granddad believes Huey's research. Ruckus and Granddad say "bullshit" at the same time.

In the end, the "Catcher Freeman" episode does not disclose historical truth or discovery but rather how each historical voice clings to the story that best fits his perspective on social reality. Such cynicism is evidence of the fact that individuals compose history, and all individuals can frame history in the name of a larger social good while actually affirming themselves. At the episode's end, Riley makes up his own story, where Catcher Freeman looks like the star in a hip-hop rap video, with fancy cars, women, and jewelry. But this was Riley's episode all along; his comedic interruptions have positioned him as the most active listener, who enjoyed the racist script, decried the romantic one, and ignored the truth. While we imagine ourselves with Huey's rational clarity, we're all really Riley clothed in Huey's evenhanded presentation. While they share in the stories they all stay radically differentiated and molded in individual perspectives. Each realizes his own truth personally and remains locked within it except for, paradoxically, in the connection and community of the storytelling.

There are three phrases during the episode that strike at the significance of counterhistory's counterlife. At the end of Robert's story, Robert proclaims, "That's exactly how it happened." Against the background of Robert screaming about the lies in Uncle Ruckus's version, Ruckus replies, "Robert . . . I'm just reciting the historical record." Huey, in a blurry mixture of frustration and curiosity, concludes, "We can resolve this." All these figures assume a singular digestible truth in line with their expectations. But what we get is an alternative to the alternative to the alternative. Catcher Freeman's story falls apart as a heroic narrative to be believed and followed because no one from the community can agree on its truth. There is an utter lack of consensus, but the sheer desire to be celebrated and listened to and recognized as having a voice, even if that voice is not telling truth or one's own self-interested truth, becomes the significance. Hence, we have a community that imagines itself in need of truth, without it. Or is the point that simultaneous versions of the past keep getting told and retold but never the same way twice? Complexity, unpredictability, and revision create difference even if occasioned by the same event. This dissonance unravels into the counterlife of counterhistory.

1 in 10,0000

The absurdity and profundity of Catcher Freeman and Thelma is that they were both heroes because they were willing to risk their lives to free enslaved Africans. Madison Washington took on the same challenge for himself, his wife's memory, and a community of slaves. Can an enslaved African be a radical and a hero and only serve himself and his interest? *Django Unchained* features Django, a freed slave who wreaks havoc on white plantation owners, in search of his wife who is enslaved on a plantation. Depending on how one sees it, there are a surprising number of films that feature Black cowboys, from comedies like *Blazing Saddles* (1974) to more dramatic westerns such as *Posse* (1993), *Unforgiven* (1992), or *The Magnificent Seven* (2016). There are Black people in both peripheral and major roles in westerns. Django is one of the heroes of the spaghetti western genre. There are hundreds of Djangos. What Tarantino did with *Django Unchained* is not only put a Black hero in one of the whitest forms of film, but he positioned plantation slavery as central to the film's tapestry.

This plantation tapestry for the Django series is provocative in terms of aesthetic risks and experimentation. Tarantino takes a beloved popular category and mixes it with a subject that progressives routinely describe as repressed. But is this a slavery story of revenge and rescue, one of Black freedom, or both? When it comes to what we expect from Black heroes, there is a fundamental opposition between the individualistic iconography of the American western and the communal sacrifice of the enslaved African hero. This tension points to a crisis of identity between who can be a Black hero or what defines a Black hero in slave texts, and I find *Django* an exemplar precisely because it dramatizes the significance of this question without resolving it. This indicates the counterlife of *Django Unchained* and its importance to slave heroics and counterhistory.

What can Django's tale of heroism, Blackness, and violent revenge reveal about counterlife? Although Black villains and heroes have shot whites and other enemies in other films, it is quite unique that *Django* is a cowboy/western revenge story set in slavery. How Django claims himself, his name, his wife, and his freedom and remains the center of the film strikes of innovation and uniqueness. Django acquires skill, language, and stylistic performance, and through this he acquires wealth and revenge as an American capitalist individual. *Django* is a symbol of radical Black heroism, in form and content of presentation, yet a death-dealing bounty hunter, preeminently an American individualist that the Black hero collective combats. In other words, while Django maintains a vicious courage against white power/slave masters, as well as creative powers of reinvention, he has no home in the collective politics of abolitionism, civil rights, Black Nationalism, or Black Lives Matter. Django is Black, radical, heroic, and counterhistorical, yet he abandons what it means to be a Black masculine hero of slavery as has been discussed in this chapter.

Django's story begins when handlers are transporting him and other slaves, but the handlers turn out to be wanted men. A German (American) bounty hunter identifies the handlers and shoots them, setting the slaves free. The German and Django agree that if Django helps the German earn his living, the German will help Django find his wife. Throughout, Django advances on natural instincts, shooting, acting, and scheming in ways that he'd previously had some concept of but that clearly he begins to master. After Django fulfills his obligations to Dr. King Schultz, they go on to scheme the destruction of Candyland, where Broomhilda Von Shaft (Hildy), Django's wife, is a slave.

When Tarantino discusses his film, he recalls his fascination for blaxploitation films, which he was inspired by in the creation of his (blaxploitation) film *Jackie Brown* (1997), starring Pam Grier. Tarantino's love for Black culture and his experience being around Black music is pure. What I mean by pure is that he cares only modestly about the things Spike Lee cares about. Spike Lee, not to mention Charles Burnett and John Singleton, have more overt antiracist critiques in their films. Singleton's film *Rosewood* (1997) and Mario Van Peebles's *Posse* tell the story of forgotten all-Black towns and thousands of Black cowboys who fought for Black freedom. Singleton's and Van Peebles's films were trying to call attention to these stories that aren't widely circulated. They call attention to minor figures, others excluded from the historical record, memory, and official data.

Django will not be found as someone scrubbed from the record because of some systematic exclusion. Django is Tarantino's creation, which he celebrates as such. Django is not a noble African warrior but an opportunist bounty hunter: an American enriching himself within the confines of the law—killing the wanted in front of children and loved ones. Bounty hunting is a dirty business. Slavery is based on turning people into capital, dehumanizing them, separating loved ones and families (or keeping families together), all to serve masters' interests and profits. Being a bounty hunter is also using bodies for money. To become free, by his own choice, Django becomes a bounty hunter, a job for which he must perform, be appraised, and drive slaves.

There is a string of characters who are exceptions in this film. The film marks exceptionality in different ways. Django is the most exceptional in the film. He masters bounty hunting and shooting and just about any other difficulty he confronts. Django's wife, Hildy, is a German-speaking slave raised as a house servant in the company of a mistress. The fact that Hildy speaks German is an astonishing fact in the film. Now this is plausible, but the concept Dr. Shultz makes clear, and Django does too, is that Hildy is something almost no one has seen before. Stephen, the slave in charge of Candyland, is so close to his master that he has more influence and power in the house. He too is an exception. We learn to despise Stephen only because he is the enemy of reunification and the love plot, not because he masters the slaves on the plantation. There is some backlash for that, but the mastery of Tarantino's story is that the audience's anger comes from Stephen's hatred for Django and his epic desire to enforce authority for authority's sake.

Why does Stephen care if Hildy leaves the plantation other than for the gamesmanship of power of his master, Candy. Even Dr. Schultz's willingness to embrace, teach, mentor, and lose his life for Django is far-fetched, but the movement of the plot is fast and riveting, so his commitment to Django is understood as the right thing to do. Django is the natural genius of everything he touches, and it is his inventiveness with the skill sets he acquires that allows him to reclaim his wife. He's a sniper, ingenious plotter, and superb actor or at least a persuasive one. He embodies violence with moral purpose, not Moral purpose. He represents the American way—he is a hero without a larger cause because he is *the* cause.

There are two images that read counterintuitively, and they are perhaps the most important in the film's overall significance: first is Candyland in flames, and the other is Django and Hildy riding off on horses into the sunset. Slavery has given birth to an American hero who has mastered violence to his own ends. He has also claimed vengeance as the crux of his nobility. The audience revels in it and so is complicit. Slavery burns, but in the ruins of Candyland we do not see slaves maneuvering and organizing to become free. The notion of the heroic extends to one person: Django. But the personal depth of he is and who he is not does not matter; image matters. A Black ex-slave turned bounty hunter rides off on horseback with his German-speaking wife (who did virtually nothing to free herself)—there is no equivalent to this in American cinema.

It is difficult to name the film where a Black couple, the product of a Black man's redemptive violence, rides out into the sunset. Django possesses her, destroys Candyland, and earned and amplified every sense of freedom he has, so that all power over him is no longer visible, but neither are his ethical and communal responsibilities. So is he a Black hero, and is his story a counterhistory in the vein of Madison Washington? The answer is clearly no. He's a neoliberal hero, an American icon in handsome blackface, but he still masters the key Black cultural tropes of the trickster and the flamboyance of decoration one can see in the beauty of 1970s blaxploitation films and the pageantry of *The Wiz* (1978).

More important, Django's counterlife stems from the fact that he is a cluster, a radical assemblage of the past and present. His ideology is still by himself, for himself, and he has no bearing on communal politics. His heroism titillates the audience with violence, vigor, and color, yet his individuality and distance from his community correspond perfectly with his lauded exceptionalism and his triumph.

Django epitomizes the Obama moment's contradictions.[28] American audiences needed to see, digest, and embrace the picturesque position of Django and Hildy. Django and Hildy's relationship to the rest of the slaves in the film is similar to the real and symbolic distance between the Obamas and the masses of Black people. Django is all kinds of Black, all kinds of beautiful neoliberal, and a particular type of anticommunal liberator, all marshaling the force of his identity. Django is a revolution in genre and image, and his irreverence toward Black communal politics is key to this. Hence, he forces us to ask what is radical, Black, and heroic, rather than assuming a ready-made set of values. Liberating radical double- and triple-speak defines the film's counterlife. Django is vexed and contradictory in a heroic mode that constitutes simplicity and predictability, which does not make Tarantino's filmmaking any less innovative. Django's feat and counterlife lie in the fact that he's the last Black hero.

Hidden Figures

All histories can be alternative histories. Counterhistories upset established points of view from the topic, style, and effect of accepted normative history or other counterhistories. In the traditional mode of Black hero, in works from Garnet's call to arms to Marvel's *Black Panther* (2018), there is something moving to American audiences about the heroic—sometimes disturbing (even destructive) and other times uplifting. It is sweetest when it is with both provocative and profound clashes. Douglass's *Heroic Slave*, McGruder's "Catcher Freeman," and Tarantino's *Django Unchained* are all counterhistories to established and accepted heroism with a Black masculine hero. More provocatively, they open different avenues that decenter the Black hero and call attention to women and ordinary slaves that may not be heroic but are crucially necessary, demanding more historical investigation and storytelling. What is more, this genre's goal is truth, revelation, new consciousness, and action on behalf of rebellious antiracist narratives, but these texts about enslaved Africans do much more wrangling in contradiction, enigma, and competing aims and perspectives. One is left thinking, is there one type of Black hero, and what makes him Black? Once we've accepted him, do we need him any longer?

It is not enough to remember, or not forget, to be a hero, but counterhistories proliferate counterhistories rather than solve problems and verify outcomes, and this is part of their inspirational purpose. Thus, the counterlife of counterhistory is a refusal to be singular, itself, and it remains unsettled, fraught, opposed, and different in that conflict again and again. There may not be traction, but there certainly is profundity worthy of inquiry repeated and often.

In the film *Hidden Figures* (2016), we learn about three Black women engineers and computer scientists in a NASA program of white men. They became heroes. But this film leads to a nameless group of computational experts called machines. The dehumanization of that task is part of the film's tactical brilliance. We know nothing about them, and their work is arduous. They were named and nameless, not necessarily fighting to end segregation, and yet their everyday lives under Jim Crow were just as precious and complex as those of the players thrust into the limelight. Curiosity about the living machine's counterhistory produces new lines of thought and representation. These women did not enter history through a conflict with the law or a major political event but on the winds of counterhistory. *Hidden Figures* is not just about being unknown; it's about being enigmatic. Divulging its counterlife means being a witness to how it repairs a record and also destabilizes identities and destroys them.

CODA

Chasing Ghosts

Death had found them watching, trying to see beyond seeing.
—Zora Neale Hurston, *Their Eyes Were Watching God*

The Chartres Cathedral symbolizes Western art and civilization. It has
nothing to do with transatlantic slavery. It is a massive and beautiful structure that Henry Adams famously admired for its most impressive "measure
of human depth" in its religious art and architecture.[1] James Baldwin walked
into the very same cathedral. He wrote: "The cathedral at Chartres . . .
says something to the people of this village which it cannot say to me; but it
is important to understand that this cathedral says something to me which
it cannot say to them."[2] Baldwin's observation is one of belonging and difference. Toni Morrison's reflections on Baldwin made her think about inhabiting a space when one does not have a claim to it.[3] Frank Wilderson
would likely agree with Morrison's thinking here, attributing Baldwin's
meditation to his ontological exclusion from humanity brought about by
transatlantic slavery.[4]

The fact that slavery sticks with us shapes Baldwin's view of why the Chartres Cathedral speaks differently to him. Wilderson, interestingly enough, contends that in Baldwin's, Morrison's, and even in our own moment, "slavery is cathedralized."[5] Slavery is modernity's Chartres. I stay with this figuration because it connects with my initial problem with Stanley Elkins's closed system or Max Weber's iron cage; it gives the impression of a static relation of material and ideological inputs/outputs (and their dialectics) and closes off the idea that Baldwin's relationship to the cathedral, his slave ancestry, his exclusion and inclusion as a person in the West, and the weight of that reality on him has a locatable singular root and discernable trajectory. As much a student of himself as Baldwin was, it is not clear that he ever believed that slavery, which was no singular act or object, was the source through which every waking modern thought must be funneled. That is, because slavery defines Blackness and Blackness defines modernity, it also means that slavery is not one of many factors but *the* factor through which all of Baldwin's expression can be best explained.

My claim in this book about counterlife relies on a belief that social experience and ontological categories remain in constant flux, contradiction, unmooring. If we imagine slavery as a cathedral of horror, to account for slavery's counterlife, we have to think of Chartres speaking to Baldwin and him speaking back in layered thoughts and memories, in dreams remembered and nightmares forgotten—powerful and profound—without or beyond immediate political utility. Engaging with slavery's presence means turning it into a question and being willing to repeatedly ask why we are starting with the answer. Because asking this question, by itself, is admission of a multitude of answers, so many of which are beyond our reach as critics. Slavery's cathedral, in our minds, archives, and expression, is multiple, moving, and awake, and most of all it is uncanny. Does that mean that we are haunted by slavery and its ungraspable ghosts?

Some scholars ask without fatigue: is slavery still with us? Whether slavery is or is not with us is a question that I don't find interesting. No doubt, slavery is still with us. The interesting question is how is slavery still with us? If slavery is a sinful ghost, is an exorcism possible? What I have tried to show in this book is partially dictated by the explosion of references to slavery in scholarship, museum displays, film, and fiction, not to mention political references because of slavery's connection to prison reform. But does that mean we are haunted by it or freer in our engagement with slavery as history and with the creation of slave texts? I submit that the complexity and vibrancy of our contemporary moment exemplifies the counterlife of enslaved Africans.

In *Playing in the Dark* (1992), Morrison emphasized slavery's uncanny influences on the nation's "racial unconsciousness."[6] From Harriet Jacobs to William Faulkner to Kara Walker, the most celebrated texts of American art reflect slavery's horrific scenes. While no one could deny the presence of slavery on the minds of progressive activists, poets, and the audience for the miniseries *Roots* (1977), in the decades prior to Morrison's *Playing*, American literary scholars all too seldom discussed slavery, even while it was clear to historians and sociologists how much slavery mattered. One could even say that the failure or reluctance to recognize the centrality of slavery by Americanists provoked Morrison's assertion that slavery's effects still have yet to be fully grasped. Nor was Morrison alone in making this critique: in an infamous speech at Howard University in 1994, vitriolic Black activist Khalid Muhammad remarked on the presence of a Jewish Holocaust Museum and the absence of a public memorial recognizing the millions of slaves who died in the Middle Passage. However offensive Muhammad's speech, like the arguments of Morrison and many other scholars and artists, it presents slavery's Holocaust as a living present that Americans generally do not want to face. David Marriott puts it another way, observing that the United States has failed to mourn slavery, and thus slavery maintains a haunting occult presence, "nowhere but nevertheless everywhere."[7]

Invoking slavery as a ghost, as Avery Gordon explains, is not a capacious haunting that encompasses a "generalizable social phenomenon," but something more specific; slavery's haunting is a "repressed or unresolved social violence making itself known."[8] Actually, Gordon mischaracterizes the agency of slavery since it is not the haunting subject but the critic that makes "it" known, and in thinking about the previous examples of Morrison, Muhammad, or Marriott, the critic or activist makes the haunting known implicitly or explicitly on behalf of someone or something. The discloser of slavery's haunting enlists and rallies history and memory for a cause. The cause demands for institutions and individuals to publicly recognize and include slavery where it was previously ignored or excluded.

While one might surmise what could have been the broader impact of well-intentioned public reckonings, museums, or presidential apologies on slavery's ghosts, Americanists have made slavery and its legacies central to their work since the late 1980s. Along with upstart African American studies programs at wealthy and visible institutions, there was a surge in writing on slavery by Morrison, Charles Johnson, Gayl Jones, Fred D'Aguiar, and Octavia Butler, along with renewed attention to the significance of slave narratives and other forms of Black culture in their diasporic, transnational, and regional iterations. Currently, there is no shortage of slavery texts to look at or discuss, and scholars are still overturning even more. With a heightened scholarly awareness and institutional support, the discourse of slavery might not be everywhere in the twentieth and twenty-first centuries, but it is certainly not hard to find.

Slavery is no longer the outlier, no longer peculiar; confronting and analyzing it is the status quo. Encouraged by a groundswell of critics unveiling the routine violence and trauma of slavery, scholars still eagerly draw on the diction of a hidden and unconscious haunting—deploying ghosts, shadows, Blackness, darkness, horror, terror, and subjection, and all guises of death (civil, social, etc.). On the one hand, almost no one denies the myriad of opportunities to call dramatically on the history of slavery, yet many critics insist that it is hidden, a ghostly occasion for thinking that discloses the highly adaptable racism always lying in wait. Still, slavery scholars in American studies have been involved in interrogating the indubitable presence of what Salamishah Tillet calls "sites of slavery": memories, material objects, events, locations, and experiences related to chattel slavery.[9] Tillet's attention to diverse sites not only surpasses the study of Black writers, but her eclecticism expands the broader American literary terrain established by groundbreaking essay collections like *Slavery and the Literary Imagination* (1989). With this in mind, scholars can no longer characterize slavery as a haunting repression whose subjugated knowledge awaits daylight and freedom. I propose that slavery scholars abandon the rubric of a repressed haunting and recast slavery as the opposite: uninhibited proliferation.

Whether one conceptualizes modernity through the history of capitalism, agriculture, and trade or through literacy and science, one cannot escape the pervasive discourse on the African slave trade and slavery. Recent studies on the role of slavery in the formation of European civilization and aesthetic taste, modern technology and commodity culture, as well as reason and literacy, demonstrate the advancing proliferation and visibility of slavery texts. Indeed, keeping the notion that slavery is haunting and repressed stifles the way critics can understand the new directions that analysts of slavery are taking. In not realizing haunting as an outmoded way to view slavery, critics risk misrecognizing the distinctiveness of the present moment of slavery discourse. Even more important, when critics invoke haunting for its rhetorical and political effect, it obscures how various sites of slave performances demand the currency of new rubrics, historical, personal, and political—some of which are currently being done by critics yet still need to be further explored, exploited, and critiqued.

Whether conceiving of modernity as technology and mechanization, the culture of taste, or literacy, there has been a proliferation of slavery texts and intertexts—an abundant, vibrant discourse of slavery in its own moment but especially in the last three decades. While some of these critical works rely on the rhetoric of haunting or repression, the vitality and profundity of their visibility and subject matter undermine those very claims. They participate not in a constricting and concealing field of discourse but in a widening discussion of slavery, which further elaborates how slavery is reproduced, analyzed, and disseminated in various contested views of modernity. Critics should address the need to reconcile the historical fact that slavery shaped the present but only to do so with a stern willingness to distinguish it completely from other more pressing forms of contemporary racial injustice.

We are not haunted by slavery, but there is something broader in haunting that is useful in our scholarly engagement with slave texts. For haunting is a rubric that encourages critics to engage historical objects that disrupt individuals in unforeseen ways. There is little by way of predicting or assuming this a priori. If we fully credit this sense of unpredictability, we are returned to a contradiction that counterlife exemplifies. Counterlife's simultaneity makes no substantive use of ghosts and specters, yet this analysis evokes what is vital to haunting if it is to be used at all in terms of slavery: personal risk, uncertainty, and vulnerability, or put differently, situations where subjects are divorced from the clarity, mastery, and freedom that they believe shields them from forces they cannot control. This social and psychological reality, too, is central to modernity and slavery. As scholars fascinated by the study of slavery, we should embrace more curiosity and uncertainty as we stumble into archives and texts we have neglected or ignored, and perhaps we will reveal them and ourselves in ways we have never expected.

INTRODUCTION

1. Morrison, *Playing in the Dark*, 37.

2. J. H. Franklin, *From Slavery to Freedom*; Patterson, *Slavery and Social Death*; Patterson, *Freedom*; Hegel, *Phenomenology of Spirit*; Jacobs, *Incidents in the Life of a Slave Girl*; and Turner, *Confessions of Nat Turner, the Leader of the Late Insurrection in Southampton, Va.* (1831), artistically rendered in William Styron's novel *The Confessions of Nat Turner* (1967) and Nate Parker's film *The Birth of a Nation* (2016).

3. An Oscar-nominated documentary titled *13th* (dir. Ava DuVernay) captures this set of questions about how white supremacy and labor demands kept Black people in shackles of coercion. There is probably no one more erudite on this concept than Saidiya Hartman. Her work exemplifies the phrase "the afterlife of slavery." There are too many scholars to list, from legal and pragmatic to the historical and theoretical, who believe and contest that slavery triumphantly reaches its tentacles beyond its burial in 1865. I've selected Hartman and a few others for reference here. See Hartman, *Scenes of Subjection*; Hartman, *Lose Your Mother*; Sharpe, *Monstrous Intimacies*; Wagner, *Disturbing the Peace*; and Blackmon, *Slavery by Another Name*.

4. Elkins, *Slavery: An Intellectual History*; Genovese, *Roll, Jordan, Roll*; Blassingame, *Slave Community*; L. Levine, *Black Culture and Black Consciousness*; Stuckey, *Slave Culture*; Holt, *Problem of Freedom*; White, *Ar'n't I a Woman*; Stevenson, *Life in Black and White*; Berlin, *Many Thousands Gone*; Gikandi, *Slavery and the Culture of Taste*; Patterson, *Slavery and Social Death*; Baucom, *Specters of the Atlantic*; Smallwood, *Saltwater Slavery*; Wilson, *Specters of Democracy*; Copeland, *Bound to Appear*; Snyder, *Power to Die*; V. Brown, *The Reaper's Garden*; W. Johnson, *Soul by Soul*; Gilroy, *Black Atlantic*; Cobb, *Picture Freedom*.

5. See Newman, *Go Down, Moses*, 106.

6. For more interpretive differences and strategies on slave religious thought and culture, see Armstrong, *Logic of Slavery*; Young, *Grey Album*; Patterson,

Slavery and Social Death; Hartman, *Scenes of Subjection*; Stuckey, *Slave Culture*; and L. Levine, *Black Culture and Black Consciousness*.

7. Armstrong, *Logic of Slavery*; Young, *Grey Album*; Patterson, *Slavery and Social Death*; Hartman, *Scenes of Subjection*; Stuckey, *Slave Culture*; L. Levine, *Black Culture and Black Consciousness*.

8. J. A. Brown, "I, John, Saw the Holy Number."

9. Ellison, "Art of Fiction," 214–15.

10. Roth, *The Counterlife*, 232.

11. Roth, *The Counterlife*, 232.

12. Brent Hayes Edwards discusses the interest in objects that exceed "the usual categories" as a "queer practice of the archive." See Edwards, "Taste of the Archive," 970.

13. Baldwin, "Everybody's Protest Novel"; also see Baldwin, "Many Thousands Gone."

14. Ellis, "New Black Aesthetic."

15. Golden, "Thelma Golden by Glenn Ligon."

16. When Gilles Deleuze and Félix Guattari discuss the rhizome, they write in similar terms: establish "a logic of the AND . . . do away with foundations, nullify endings and beginnings." See Deleuze and Guattari, *A Thousand Plateaus*, 25.

17. Gutman, *The Black Family*, 335.

18. Baptist and Camp, "Introduction," 3; W. Johnson, *River of Dark Dreams*, 9. See also D. Jones, "Fruit of Abolition"; and V. Brown, "Social Death and Political Life."

19. English, *How to See a Work*, 75.

20. David Scott, *Conscripts of Modernity*, 7–8.

21. Best, *None Like Us*, 23, 63.

22. David Scott, *Conscripts of Modernity*, 13. I also think Christopher Hager's book *Word by Word* begins to do some of the work of abandoning older critical paradigms, but this book focuses more on freed slaves and does not fully grapple with the critical and historical strictures of slavery studies particular to this conversation. I feel similarly about David Kazanjian's *Brink of Freedom*, which also leans toward freedom's philosophical expression in comparative contexts rather than specifically rethinking slavery's. I am more invested in unwinding slavery/ freedom altogether (or as much as possible) than Kazanjian's project. I see my claims in this book as part of a broader conversation with these important books.

23. Brooks, *Bodies in Dissent*, 10.

24. McMillan, *Embodied Avatars*, 60. Also see McKittrick, *Demonic Grounds*; and Browne, *Dark Matters*.

25. McMillan, *Embodied Avatars*, 9.

26. Brooks, *Bodies in Dissent*, 10.

27. Best, *None Like Us*, 63. See also Helton et al., "The Question of Recovery," 125; Rusert, "Disappointment in the Archives of Black Freedom"; and J. Ferguson, "Race and the Rhetoric of Resistance."

28. Trouillot, "The Otherwise Modern," 234.

29. Fleetwood, "Posing in Prison." Fleetwood's work on carceral intimacy is a refreshing and nuanced take on the narrative, image, and emotional labor that illuminate the ongoing work of social life in the most tragic and coercive conditions.

30. See Best, "Unfit for History"; Best's thinking, forming, and deforming the way we contemplate slave texts resonates in my thinking here.

31. B. Brown, "Reification, Reanimation, and the American Uncanny."

32. Bandele, discussion of *When They Call You a Terrorist*.

33. Bandele, discussion of *When They Call You a Terrorist*.

34. David Scott, *Stuart Hall's Voice*, 19.

35. David Scott, *Stuart Hall's Voice*, 27.

36. Campt, *Listening to Images*, 6.

37. Campt, *Listening to Images*, 6.

38. Hurston, *Their Eyes Were Watching God*, 7.

39. Haley, *No Mercy Here*, 110.

40. Hurston, *Their Eyes Were Watching God*, 192.

1. SAMBO'S CLOAK

1. Baldwin, "Everybody's Protest Novel," 33.

2. Angela Davis, interviewed in *Democracy Now*, "'Toni Morrison Will Always Be with Us.'"

3. Davis, *Women, Race, and Class*, 4.

4. For scholarship on the debates about slavery, Black urban life, and the emergence of the social sciences, see R. A. Ferguson, *Aberrations in Black*; David Scott, *Contempt and Pity*; King, *Race, Culture, and the Intellectuals*; and Warren, *So Black and Blue*.

5. Murray, *The Omni-Americans*, 39.

6. Best, *None Like Us*, 72. Best locates the origins of "recovery" scholarship with the publication of John Blassingame's *Slave Community* (1979), and here's where he runs into why I think Elkins's work and the loud responses to it (as well as appropriations of it) remain a critical flashpoint. Blassingame's archival readings and conceptual work in *Slave Community* were primarily aimed at disputing Elkins's "slave personality"/Sambo thesis, which Blassingame directly and indirectly refers to throughout. Furthermore, the ethical and political recovery movement Best identifies goes back at least to Kenneth Stampp's *The Peculiar Institution* (1967). At the same time, Best indubitably demonstrates that *Beloved* had a galvanizing and catalytic effect, by itself an event (as Davis describes it in her way) that substantially changed slavery studies in much of the way Best claims.

7. Best, *None Like Us*, 63.

8. Best, *None Like Us*, 78.

9. Best, *None Like Us*, 65.

10. There are other varieties of thinking about time/progress (or refusing to) besides forward and backward. Some scholars emphasize master/slave relations as always vacillating between poles or pockets of power, indicating a kind of ongoing stagnancy or tug-of-war. I still think that despite shifts in lexicon or time concepts most discussions are framed explicitly or implicitly to identify that transformations for equality constitute forward movement and worsening conditions/treatment/exclusions constitute a step back or a failure to create necessary change.

11. Christopher Marlowe referenced Helen's inspirational visage in *Dr. Faustus* (1604): "Was this the face that launched a thousand ships?" (223). In a similar spirit, President Abraham Lincoln said about Harriet Beecher Stowe: so, it was you "who wrote the book that started this great war." Quoted in Wilson, *Patriotic Gore*, 3.

12. Elkins, *Slavery*, 81.

13. White, *Ar'n't I a Woman?*, 8–9.

14. White, *Ar'n't I a Woman?*, 8.

15. The study of slaves and their cultures is fundamentally defined by enduring oppositions between slaves' actions to acquire power and masters keeping it from them. Vincent Brown and Walter Johnson explain that, whether implied or directly stated, the oppositional abstractions that shape American slavery studies remain central to current critical discussions. Across a variety of periods, geographies, and contexts, scholars reveal the cultural niceties of slaves' performances, efforts to gain political leverage, and strategies of self-education, as well as other modes of self-fashioning. Paul Gilroy unveils slaves' individual self-fashioning in Black Atlantic cultures; in a review of Gilroy's book, a suspicious Colin Dayan asks, "What is this agency?" Lawrence Levine, Eric Sundquist, and Sterling Stuckey contend that slave folktales, singing, and worship contain the nascent origins of Black Nationalism and politics. Saidiya Hartman argues the opposite: slave performances do not indicate oppositional culture. For Hartman, slave expressive culture reinforces masters' coercive powers. One cannot deny that key terms like *agency* have helped scholars locate and articulate the richness of slaves' resistance and the elastic power of slavery's regimes. It appears that scholars view the field of slavery, imaginatively and literarily, as if the people and groups who inhabit it should be viewed on an escalator, either moving forward for progress or backward toward intensifying coercion and restraint. See Gilroy, *Black Atlantic*, 40; Dayan, "Paul Gilroy's Slaves, Ships, and Routes," 13; L. Levine, *Black Culture and Black Consciousness*; Sundquist, *To Wake the Nations*; Stuckey, *Slave Culture*; and Hartman, *Scenes of Subjection*. See also Brooks, *Bodies in Dissent*; Hahn, *A Nation under Our Feet*; W. Johnson, *Soul by Soul*; and Williams, *Self-Taught*. For more recent work on agency's significance to slavery and political thinking, see Roberts, *Freedom as Marronage*; and Raboteau, *Slave Religion*.

16. Weber, *Protestant Ethic*, 181.

17. Huyssen, *Miniature Metropolis*, 22.

18. Phillips, *American Negro Slavery*.

19. Elkins, *Slavery*, 23; Stampp, *Peculiar Institution*.

20. Elkins, *Slavery*, 224.

21. Elkins, *Slavery*, 23.

22. Elkins, *Slavery*, 223.

23. Lane, *Debate over Slavery*.

24. Elkins, *Slavery*, 270.

25. Adams, *Education of Henry Adams*, 1035.

26. Adams, *Education of Henry Adams*, 1035.

27. Adams, *Education of Henry Adams*, 1035.

28. Martin, *Harvests of Change*, 3.

29. Martin, *Harvests of Change*, 11.

30. See Seltzer, *Bodies and Machines*.

31. Weber, *Protestant Ethic*, 180. The most recent translation is highly critical of the "iron cage" translation, but the effect of the "iron cage," however hotly debated as of late, has had staying power and is still undeniable and quite useful.

32. Mills and Gerth, *Character and Social Structure*, 22–23. See also Riesman, Glazer, and Denney, *Lonely Crowd*.

33. Adorno, Frenkel-Brunswik, Levinson, and Sanford, *Authoritarian Personality*, 11.

34. Whyte, *Organization Man*, 32.

35. Riesman, Glazer, and Denney, *Lonely Crowd*, 30.

36. Elkins opened his discussion of slave personality with a basic question: "Was he [Sambo] real or unreal?" (*Slavery*, 62). Elkins launched his inquiry with the belief that whites in 1860s believed that Sambo was the "dominant plantation type" (62). Elkins's accounting stayed true to accounting for Sambo's existence rather than dismissing his existence altogether. Elkins did not set out to prove Sambo is true but rather to wager his existence with scientific clarity and historical understanding as a way to register it as the social reality of slave personality. If one could think of something that Southern apologists agree on, it is the existence of Sambo. Sambo appeared in minstrel shows, television shows, children's stories, cartoons, and film. Sambo is a crucial part of Southern lore, culture, and material culture. Spike Lee's film *Bamboozled* (2000) captured the problem with Sambo in that he is purely the construction of how whites perceive, imitate, and distort Black life and culture for profit and entertainment. Black people exist for this purpose: to serve whites' interests in entertainment, labor, and other areas of domination. Sambo is the Negro Southern whites wish to see and remember. Sambo was a key player on laundry lists of racist stereotypes. The Sambo figure is not necessarily named Sambo, but he plays the role of the cheerful, subservient entertainer, sometimes clever or lazy, and even slightly disruptive, but ultimately safely under the thumb of whites in power.

37. Frazier, *Negro Family*; Park, *Race and Culture*.

38. Elkins borrowed from Frank Tannenbaum's *Slave and Citizen* (1946), which claimed that Latin American slavery had no system governing it all and that US slavery's system was fixed. Latin America, as a crucial antecedent, had no horizontal plane of division—and because of this, free internal adaptations between free and unfree marriage, religion, emancipation. The United States' social legal codes for slavery, while varying across states, were rigid and protected masters against slave social and political interests. Hence while Stampp insisted on slaves resisting and detesting slavery, Stampp also claimed that slaves maintained a great many personalities and types. Elkins questioned how Tannenbaum could be right about a fixed system that produces an abundant variety of persons. Elkins claimed the closed system of slavery, while appearing to produce a surface of variety, proved ultimately to be Sambo's because the only people that rebelled against slavery were figures exposed to aspects outside of it. Hence, the lack of revolts from antebellum plantations reduced enslaved Africans, who for a variety of reasons succumbed to it. Tannenbaum, *Slave and Citizen*, 106.

39. Wright, "How Bigger Was Born," 443.

40. Elkins, *Slavery*, 104.

41. Elkins, *Slavery*, 106.

42. Bourke-White, "The Liberation of Buchenwald."

43. Elkins, *Slavery*, 126.

44. Elkins, *Slavery*, 139.

45. Elkins, *Slavery*, 137.

46. Althusser, "Ideology and Ideological State Apparatuses," 127–28.

47. See Dayan, *Law Is a White Dog*; Cacho, *Social Death*; and DeLombard, *In the Shadow of the Gallows*.

48. V. Brown, "Social Death and Political Life." I discuss Brown's position at length in *Melville and the Idea of Blackness*, 99.

49. Patterson, *Slavery and Social Death*, 13.

50. Patterson, *Slavery and Social Death*, 100.

51. Patterson, *Slavery and Social Death*, 101.

52. Patterson, *Slavery and Social Death*, 101.

53. See, for example, Sharpe, *Monstrous Intimacies*; and Wilderson, *Red, White and Black*.

54. Hartman, *Scenes*, 14.

55. Hartman, *Scenes*, 52.

56. Hartman, *Scenes*, 52.

57. White, *Ar'n't I a Woman?*, 8.

58. David Scott, *Conscripts of Modernity*, 111.

59. Elkins, *Slavery*, 277.

60. Ellison, "A Very Stern Discipline," 736.

61. Ellison, "A Very Stern Discipline," 737.

62. Genovese, *Roll, Jordan, Roll*, 617.

63. Patterson, "Peculiar Institution Again," 37.

64. Patterson, "Peculiar Institution Again," 37.

65. V. Brown, "Social Death and Political Life," 1246.

66. Berlin, *Many Thousands Gone*, 13.

67. Berlin, *Many Thousands Gone*, 2, 3. There is a theoretical analogue to Berlin's historical insight in my concept of "epistemic estrangement," which I mention in the previous section on "counterlife." See Freeburg, *Black Aesthetics*, 3.

68. Berlin, *Many Thousands Gone*, 13.

69. Tavia Nyong'o captures the spirt of what I'm after with counterlife in this sentence: "Rather than refuse the death drive that inspirits such discourses . . . I propose a speculative method of decrypting Blackness that would dive into that drive, divine its agencies and energies, and provide a fuller account of the ambitious consequence of living with its regnant influence." See Nyong'o, *Afro-Fabulations*, 203.

2. KALEIDOSCOPE VIEWS

1. Baldwin, "Of the Sorrow Songs," 124.

2. Douglass's shadow looms large. Some scholars warn of Douglass's overweight in slavery studies; see, for example, Drexler and White, eds., *Beyond Douglass*.

3. Douglass, *Narrative of the Life*, 65.

4. Douglass, *My Bondage*, 282.

5. Douglass, *My Bondage*, 287.

6. Douglass, *Narrative*, 63.

7. Douglass, *Narrative*, 63.

8. Douglass, *Narrative*, 64.

9. Douglass, *Narrative*, 65.

10. Douglass, *My Bondage*, 281.

11. Douglass, *My Bondage*, 281.

12. Douglass, *My Bondage*, 279.

13. Douglass, *My Bondage*, 282.

14. Douglass, *My Bondage*, 283.

15. Douglass, *My Bondage*, 282.

16. Du Bois, *The Souls of Black Folk*, 497–98.

17. Chireau, *Black Magic*, 13, 21; Raboteau, *Slave Religion*, 280.

18. Raboteau, *Slave Religion*, 275

19. Gilroy, *Black Atlantic*, 62.

20. Gilroy, *Black Atlantic*, 62.

21. Douglass, *Narrative*, 65.

22. Freeburg, *Black Aesthetics*, 3.

23. I call this known/unknown purely because of the self/other distinction of "epistemic estrangement." See Freeburg, *Black Aesthetics*, 3.

24. Jones, *Known World*, 384.

25. Jones, *Known World*, 296.

26. Jones, *Known World*, 12.

27. Jones, *Known World*, 295.

28. Jones, *Known World*, 295.

29. Jones, *Known World*, 296.

30. Jones, *Known World*, 385.

31. Jones, *Known World*, 384.

32. Jones, *Known World*, 385.

33. Jones, *Known World*, 385.

34. Jones, *Known World*, 386.

35. Jones, *Known World*, 381.

36. Jones, *Known World*, 385.

37. Bailey, "Radcliffe Bailey."

38. When I think of Bailey's use of space and color in his installations, I recall a wonderful line from Judith Madera's *Black Atlas* when she writes about art (literary) as "openings of different forms of actualization" (4).

39. Diawara, "One World under the Groove," 138.

40. Diawara, "One World under the Groove," 140.

41. Copeland, *Bound to Appear*, 22.

42. Copeland, *Bound to Appear*, 10.

43. Bailey, "Radcliffe Bailey."

44. K. J. Brown, *The Repeating Body*, 141.

45. Morrison, *Beloved*, 91–94.

46. Hartman, *Lose Your Mother*, 50.

47. Bailey, "Radcliffe Bailey."

48. Diawara, "One World under the Groove," 136.

49. NOLA.com, "Radcliffe Bailey's Stunning 'Windward Coast.'"

50. Bailey, "Radcliffe Bailey."

51. Sharpe, *In the Wake*, 60–61.

52. Sharpe, *In the Wake*, 62

53. Quoted in Sharpe, *In the Wake*, 62.

54. Sharpe, *In the Wake*, 62.

55. Sharpe, *In the Wake*, 62.

56. Sambira, "The Historic 'Ark of Return' Monument."

57. Ellison, "Little Man at Chehaw Station," 509.

3. SOUNDS OF BLACKNESS

1. S. Brown, "Negro Folk Expression: Spirituals, Seculars, Ballads and Work Songs," 263.

2. W. W. Brown, "A Lectured Delivered," 4, 11.

3. Spillers, "Mama's Baby, Papa's Maybe," 206. Alexander Weheliye deploys Spillers's concept of the flesh and racialization as way to re-envision Black feminist theory, humanism, and their impacts. See *Habeas Viscus*.

4. Spillers, "Mama's Baby, Papa's Maybe," 206.

5. Spillers, "Mama's Baby, Papa's Maybe," 208.

6. Baldwin, "Of the Sorrow Songs," 124.

7. Moten, *In the Break*, 6.

8. Hurston, "Spirituals and Neo-Spirituals"; J. W. Johnson, "O Black and Unknown Bards"; Reagon, "Songs are Free."

9. See B. Brown, *Other Things*.

10. B. Brown, "Reification, Reanimation, and the American Uncanny."

11. Freeburg, *Black Aesthetics*, 43.

12. Baldwin, "Of the Sorrow Songs," 123.

13. W. W. Brown, "Lectured Delivered," 4.

14. W. W. Brown, "Lecture Delivered," 6.

15. W. W. Brown, "Lectured Delivered," 11.

16. W. Johnson, *Soul by Soul*, 176–77.

17. W. Johnson, *Soul by Soul*, 119.

18. W. Johnson, *Soul by Soul*, 119.

19. McInnis, *Slaves Waiting for Sale*, 7.

20. McInnis, *Slaves Waiting for Sale*, 6.

21. Quoted in McInnis, *Slaves Waiting for Sale*, 6; originally in "Exhibition of the Royal Academy," *Art Journal*, n.s., 7 (June 1, 1861): 165.

22. Kopytoff, "Cultural Biography of Things," 64–65.

23. Kopytoff, "Cultural Biography of Things," 65, 66.

24. Young, *Grey Album*, 67.

25. Lincoln and Mamiya, *The Black Church*, 353.

26. Higginson, *Army Life*, 188.

27. Olmsted, *A Journey*, 26.

28. Olmsted, *A Journey*, 27.

29. Smith quoted in Raboteau, *Slave Religion*, 243.

30. Raboteau, *Slave Religion*, 243.

31. Raboteau, *Slave Religion*, 245.

32. See Murphy, "Singing and Praying Bands."

33. Douglass, *Narrative*, 23.

34. Douglass, *Narrative*, 24.

35. Jacobs, *Incidents in the Life*, 518–19.

36. Douglass, *Narrative*, 23–24.

37. Du Bois, *Souls of Black Folk*, 494.

38. Hurston, "Spirituals and Neo-Spirituals," 869.

39. Hurston, "Spirituals and Neo-Spirituals," 870.

40. Raboteau, *Slave Religion*, 246.

41. Hurston, "Spirituals and Neo-Spirituals," 871.

42. Hurston, "Spirituals and Neo-Spirituals," 871.

43. Bremer, quoted in Lovell, *Black Song*, 107–8.

44. A. Franklin, "Precious Lord (Part 2)."

45. J. Brown, MLK keynote. Brown is a scholar of spirituals whose work is best evidenced in *To Stand on the Rock*.

46. J. W. Johnson, "Preface: Book of Spirituals," 739.

47. Baldwin, *Go Tell It on the Mountain*, 212.

48. Reagon, interview, *Bill Moyers Journal*.

49. Aretha Franklin Performance at White House 2015, April 16, 2015, https://www.youtube.com/watch?v=_ddYfaRuVGAo.

50. Manigault-Bryant, *Talking to the Dead*, 171.

51. Douglass, *Narrative*, 24.

4. THE LAST BLACK HERO

1. Funkenstein, *Theology and the Scientific Imagination*, 273. The work of Catherine Gallagher and Stephen Greenblatt has been helpful to my formulations. See Gallagher and Greenblatt, *Practicing New Historicism*.

2. Best, "On Failing to Make," 453.

3. Benjamin, "On the Concept of History," 390. Also see Ernest, *Liberation Historiography*.

4. Hartman, "Venus in Two Acts," 14. Hartman's full words are as follows: "However, the *history* of black counter-historical projects is one of failure, precisely because these accounts have never been able to install themselves as history, but rather are insurgent, disruptive narratives that are marginalized and derailed before they ever gain a footing."

5. Michaels, *Shape of the Signifier*, 168.

6. Garnet, "Address to the Slaves of the United States," April 15, 1848, 7. No exact transcript exists of the original address from 1843, but it was reprinted five years later with a preface from the author.

7. Garnet, "Address," 8.

8. Nate Parker interview with *Hollywood Reporter* promoting the film.

9. Ellison, "A Very Stern Discipline."

10. Garnet, "Address," 9.

11. Douglass, *Heroic Slave*, 4.

12. Douglass, *Heroic Slave*, 37.

13. See Freeburg, *Black Aesthetics*, 3.

14. Douglass, *Heroic Slave*, 42.

15. Douglass, *Heroic Slave*, 42.

16. Douglass, *Heroic Slave*, 43.

17. W. Johnson, "White Lies."

18. Douglass, *Heroic Slave*, 44.

19. Douglass, *Heroic Slave*, 47.

20. Douglass, *Heroic Slave*, 17.

21. Douglass, *Heroic Slave*, 16.

22. Douglass, *Heroic Slave*, 17.

23. Douglass, *Heroic Slave*, 17.

24. Douglass, *Heroic Slave*, 16.

25. Glymph, *Out of the House of Bondage*.

26. McGruder, "Return of the King."

27. McGruder, "The Story of Catcher Freeman."

28. Joseph Brown suggested connecting the Obama presidency to *Django Unchained* in our discussions of the film after it was released in 2012.

CODA

Parts of this chapter were originally published as "Chasing Slavery's Ghost," *American Literary History* 27, no. 1 (2015): 102–13.

1. Adams, *Education of Henry Adams*, 346; Adams, *Mont Saint Michel*.

2. Baldwin, "Stranger in the Village," 89.

3. Morrison, "City Limits, Village Values," 35.

4. Wilderson, *Red, White and Black*, 18.

5. Wilderson, *Red, White and Black*, 18.

6. Morrison, *Playing in the Dark*, xii.

7. Marriott, *Haunted Life*, xxi.

8. Gordon, *Ghostly Matters*, 8, xvi.

9. Tillet, *Sites of Slavery*, 2–4.

BIBLIOGRAPHY

Adams, Henry. *The Education of Henry Adams*. 1907; New York: Library of America, 1983.

Adams, Henry. *Mont Saint Michel and Chartres*. New York: Library of America, 1983.

Adorno, Theodor W., Else Frenkel-Brunswik, Daniel J. Levinson, and R. Nevitt Sanford. *The Authoritarian Personality, Part One*. New York: Wiley, 1964.

Althusser, Louis. "Ideology and Ideological State Apparatuses." In *Lenin and Philosophy and Other Essays*, translated by Ben Brewster, 127–86. New York: Monthly Review Press, 1971.

Armstrong, Tim. *The Logic of Slavery: Debt, Technology, and Pain in American Literature*. New York: Cambridge University Press, 2012.

Bailey, Radcliffe. "Radcliffe Bailey: Conversation with the Artist." Wellesley College, April 5, 2012. https://www.youtube.com/watch?v=m-kvAGMUXM4.

Baldwin, James. "Everybody's Protest Novel." In *The Price of the Ticket: Collected Nonfiction, 1948–1985*, 27–33. New York: St. Martin's, 1985.

Baldwin, James. *Go Tell It on the Mountain*. 1950; New York: Library of America, 1998.

Baldwin, James. "Many Thousands Gone." In *The Price of the Ticket: Collected Nonfiction, 1948–1985*, 65–78. New York: St. Martin's, 1985.

Baldwin, James. "Of the Sorrow Songs: The Cross of Redemption." In *The Cross of Redemption: Uncollected Writings*, edited by Randall Kenan, 118–24. New York: Pantheon, 2011.

Baldwin, James. *The Price of the Ticket: Collected Nonfiction, 1948–1985*. New York: St. Martin's, 1985.

Baldwin, James. "Stranger in the Village." In *The Price of the Ticket: Collected Nonfiction, 1948–1985*, 79–90. New York: St. Martin's, 1985.

Bandele, Asha, with Patrisse Khan-Cullors. Discussion of *When They Call You a Terrorist: A Black Lives Matter Memoir*. New York Public Library Podcast, February 6, 2018, episode 201. https://www.nypl.org/blog/2018/02/06/black-lives-matter-co-founder-patrisse-khan-cullors-nypl-podcast-ep-201.

Baptist, Edward E., and Stephanie M. H. Camp. "Introduction: A History of the History of Slavery in the Americas." In *New Studies in the History of American Slavery*, edited by Edward E. Baptist and Stephanie M. H. Camp, 1–20. Athens: University of Georgia Press, 2006.

Baucom, Ian. *Specters of the Atlantic: Finance Capital, Slavery, and the Philosophy of History*. Durham, NC: Duke University Press, 2005.

Benjamin, Walter. "On the Concept of History." In *Walter Benjamin, Selected Writings*, vol. 4, *1938–1940*, edited by Howard Eiland and Michael Jennings, 389–400. Cambridge, MA: Harvard University Press, 2009.

Berlin, Ira. *Many Thousands Gone: The First Two Centuries of Slavery in North America*. Cambridge, MA: Harvard University Press, 1993.

Berry, Daina Ramey. *The Price for Their Pound of Flesh: The Value of the Enslaved, from Womb to Grave, in the Building of a Nation*. Boston: Beacon, 2017.

Best, Stephen. *None Like Us: Blackness, Belonging, Aesthetic Life*. Durham, NC: Duke University Press, 2018.

Best, Stephen. "On Failing to Make the Past Present." *Modern Language Quarterly* 73, no. 3 (2012): 453–74.

Best, Stephen. "Unfit for History." Lecture, 2014, University of California, Santa Cruz. https://vimeo.com/91461686.

Blackmon, Douglas. *Slavery by Another Name: The Re-enslavement of Black Americans from the Civil War to World War II*. New York: Anchor, 2009.

Blassingame, John W. *The Slave Community: Plantation Life in the Antebellum South*. New York: Oxford University Press, 1979.

Bourke-White, Margaret. "The Liberation of Buchenwald." *Life*, May 7, 1945, 30–37.

Brooks, Daphne A. *Bodies in Dissent: Spectacular Performances of Race and Freedom, 1850–1910*. Durham, NC: Duke University Press, 2006.

Brown, Bill. *Other Things*. Chicago: University of Chicago Press, 2015.

Brown, Bill. "Reification, Reanimation, and the American Uncanny." *Critical Inquiry* 32, no. 2 (2006): 175–207.

Brown, Joseph A., S.J. "I, John, Saw the Holy Number: Apocalyptic Visions in *Go Tell It on the Mountain* and *Native Son*." *Religion and Literature* 27, no. 1 (1995): 53–74.

Brown, Joseph A., S.J. MLK keynote address at Creighton University, January 24, 2012; https://www.youtube.com/watch?v=E5lRErYM-_4.

Brown, Joseph A., S.J. *To Stand on the Rock: Meditations on Black Catholic Identity*. New York: Orbis, 1998.

Brown, Kimberly Juanita. *The Repeating Body: Slavery's Visual Resonance in the Contemporary*. Durham, NC: Duke University Press, 2015.

Brown, Sterling A. "Negro Folk Expression: Spirituals, Seculars, Ballads and Work Songs." In *A Son's Return: Selected Essays of Sterling A. Brown*, edited by Mark Sanders, 243–64. Boston: Northeastern University Press, 1996.

Brown, Vincent. *The Reaper's Garden: Death and Power in the World of Atlantic Slavery*. Cambridge, MA: Harvard University Press, 2008.

Brown, Vincent. "Social Death and Political Life in the Study of Slavery." *American Historical Review* 114, no. 5 (2009): 1231–49.

Brown, William Wells. "A Lectured Delivered before the Female Anti-slavery Society of Salem." In *The Works of William Wells Brown: Using His "Strong, Manly Voice,"* edited by Paula Garrett and Hollis Robbins, 3–18. New York: Oxford University Press, 2006.

Browne, Simone. *Dark Matters: On the Surveillance of Blackness*. Durham, NC: Duke University Press, 2015.

Cacho, Lisa Marie. *Social Death: Racialized Rightlessness and the Criminalization of the Unprotected*. New York: New York University Press, 2013.

Campt, Tina M. *Listening to Images*. Durham, NC: Duke University Press, 2017.

Chireau, Yvonne Patricia. *Black Magic: Religion and the African American Conjuring Tradition*. Berkeley: University of California Press, 2003.

Cobb, Jasmine Nichole. *Picture Freedom: Remaking Black Visuality in the Early Nineteenth Century*. New York: New York University Press, 2015.

Copeland, Huey. *Bound to Appear: Art, Slavery, and the Site of Blackness in Multicultural America*. Chicago: University of Chicago Press, 2013.

Covey, Herbert. *African American Slave Medicine: Herbal and Non-herbal Treatments*. Lanham, MD: Lexington, 2008.

Davis, Angela Y. *Women, Race, and Class*. New York: Vintage, 1981.

Dayan, Colin. *The Law Is a White Dog: How Legal Rituals Make and Unmake Persons*. Princeton, NJ: Princeton University Press, 2011.

Dayan, Joan Colin. "Paul Gilroy's Slaves, Ships, and Routes: The Middle Passage as Metaphor." *Research in African Literatures* 27, no. 4 (1996): 7–14.

Deleuze, Gilles, and Félix Guattari. *A Thousand Plateaus: Capitalism and Schizophrenia*. Translated by Brian Massumi. Minneapolis: University of Minnesota Press, 1987.

DeLombard, Jeannine Marie. *In the Shadow of the Gallows: Race, Crime, and American Civic Identity*. Philadelphia: University of Pennsylvania Press, 2012.

Democracy Now. "'Toni Morrison Will Always Be with Us': Angela Davis, Nikki Giovanni, and Sonia Sanchez Pay Tribute." *Democracy Now*, August 7, 2019. https://www.democracynow.org/shows/2019/8/7.

Diawara, Manthia. "One World under the Groove." In *Radcliffe Bailey: Memory as Medicine*, edited by Carol Thompson, 135–41. New York: Prestel, 2011.

Douglass, Frederick. *Frederick Douglass: Autobiographies*. Edited by Henry Louis Gates Jr. New York: Library of America, 1994.

Douglass, Frederick. *The Heroic Slave: A Cultural and Critical Edition*. Edited by Robert S. Levine, John Stauffer, and John R. McKivigan. 1852; New Haven, CT: Yale University Press, 2015.

Douglass, Frederick. *Life and Times of Frederick Douglass*. 1881; New York: Library of America, 1994.

Douglass, Frederick. *My Bondage and My Freedom*. Edited by Henry Louis Gates Jr. 1855; New York: Library of America, 1994.

Douglass, Frederick. *Narrative of the Life of Frederick Douglass, an American Slave*. Edited by Henry Louis Gates Jr. 1845; New York: Library of America, 1994.

Drexler, Michael, and Ed White, eds. *Beyond Douglass: New Perspectives on Early African-American Literature*. Lewisburg, PA: Bucknell University Press, 2008.

Du Bois, W. E. B. *The Souls of Black Folk*. 1903; New York: Library of America, 1987.

DuVernay, Ava, dir. *13th*. Los Angeles: Kandoo Films, 2016.

Edwards, Brent Hayes. "The Taste of the Archive." *Callaloo* 35, no. 4 (2012): 944–72.

Elkins, Stanley. *Slavery: An Intellectual History*. Chicago: University of Chicago Press, 1959.

Ellis, Trey. "The New Black Aesthetic." *Callaloo*, no. 38 (1989): 233–43.

Ellison, Ralph. "The Art of Fiction: An Interview." In *The Collected Essays of Ralph Ellison*, edited by John F. Callahan, 210–24. New York: Modern Library, 1995.

Ellison, Ralph. "The Little Man at Chehaw Station." In *The Collected Essays of Ralph Ellison*, edited by John F. Callahan, 489–519. New York: Modern Library, 1995.

Ellison, Ralph. "A Very Stern Discipline." In *The Collected Essays of Ralph Ellison*, edited by John F. Callahan, 726–54. New York: Modern Library, 1995.

English, Darby. *How to See a Work of Art in Total Darkness*. Cambridge, MA: MIT Press, 2007.

Ernest, John. *Liberation Historiography: African American Writers and Challenge of History, 1794–1861*. Chapel Hill: University of North Carolina Press, 2004.

"Exhibition of the Royal Academy," *Art Journal*, n.s., 7 (June 1, 1861): 165.

Fanon, Frantz. *Black Skin, White Masks*. Translated by Richard Philcox. 1952; New York: Grove, 2008.

Feimster, Crystal. *Southern Horrors: Women and the Politics of Rape and Lynching*. Cambridge, MA: Harvard University Press, 2009.

Ferguson, Jeffrey. "Race and the Rhetoric of Resistance." *Raritan* 28, no. 1 (2008): 4–32.

Ferguson, Roderick A. *Aberrations in Black: Toward a Queer of Color Critique*. Minneapolis: University of Minnesota Press, 2004.

Fleetwood, Nicole R. "Posing in Prison: Family Photographs, Emotional Labor, and Carceral Intimacy." *Public Culture* 27, no. 3 (2015): 487–511.

Franklin, Aretha. "Precious Lord (Part 2)." On *Songs of Faith*. Chicago: Checker Records, 1956.

Franklin, John Hope. *From Slavery to Freedom: A History of American Negroes*. New York: Knopf, 1947.

Frazier, E. Franklin. *The Negro Family in the United States.* 1939; Chicago: University of Chicago Press, 1966.

Freeburg, Christopher. *Black Aesthetics and the Interior Life.* Charlottesville: University of Virginia Press, 2017.

Freeburg, Christopher. *Melville and the Idea of Blackness: Race and Imperialism in Nineteenth-Century America.* New York: Cambridge University Press, 2012.

Funkenstein, Amos. *Theology and the Scientific Imagination: From the Middle Ages to the Seventeenth Century.* Princeton, NJ: Princeton University Press, 1986.

Gallagher, Catherine, and Stephen Greenblatt. *Practicing New Historicism.* Chicago: University of Chicago Press, 2001.

Garnet, Henry Highland. "An Address to the Slaves of the United States of America, Buffalo, N.Y., 1843." *Electronic Texts in American Studies*, 8. http://digitalcommons.unl.edu/etas/8/.

Genovese, Eugene. *Roll, Jordan, Roll: The World the Slaves Made.* New York: Vintage, 1972.

Gikandi, Simon. *Slavery and the Culture of Taste.* Princeton, NJ: Princeton University Press, 2011.

Gilroy, Paul. *The Black Atlantic: Modernity and Double Consciousness.* Cambridge, MA: Harvard University Press, 1993.

Glymph, Thavolia. *Out of the House of Bondage: The Transformation of the Plantation Household.* Cambridge: Cambridge University Press, 2008.

Golden, Thelma. "Thelma Golden by Glenn Ligon." *bomb Magazine*, April 4, 2004. http://bombmagazine.org/article/3588/thelma-golden.

Gordon, Avery. *Ghostly Matters: Haunting and the Sociological Imagination.* Minneapolis: University of Minnesota Press, 1997.

Gutman, Herbert. *The Black Family in Slavery and Freedom, 1750–1925.* New York: Pantheon, 1976.

Hager, Christopher. *Word by Word: Emancipation and the Act of Writing.* Cambridge, MA: Harvard University Press, 2013.

Hahn, Steven. *A Nation under Our Feet: Black Political Struggles in the Rural South from Slavery to the Great Migration.* Cambridge, MA: Harvard University Press, 2003.

Haley, Sarah. *No Mercy Here: Gender, Punishment, and the Making of Jim Crow Modernity.* Chapel Hill: University of North Carolina Press, 2016.

Harper, Phillip Brian. *Abstractionist Aesthetics: Artistic Form and Social Critique in African American Culture.* New York: New York University Press, 2015.

Hartman, Saidiya. "The Belly of the World: A Note on Black Women's Labors." *Souls* 18, no. 1 (2016): 166–73.

Hartman, Saidiya. *Lose Your Mother: A Journey along the Atlantic Slave Route.* New York: Farrar, Straus and Giroux, 2007.

Hartman, Saidiya V. *Scenes of Subjection: Terror, Slavery, and Self-Making in Nineteenth-Century America*. New York: Oxford University Press, 1997.

Hartman, Saidiya. "Venus in Two Acts." *Small Axe*, no. 26 (2008): 1–14.

Hartman, Saidiya. *Wayward Lives, Beautiful Experiments: Intimate Histories of Social Upheaval*. New York: Norton, 2019.

Hegel, G. W. F. *The Phenomenology of Spirit*. Translated by A. V. Miller. 1807; New York: Oxford University Press, 1977.

Helton, Laura, Justin Leroy, Max A. Mishler, Samantha Seeley, and Shauna Sweeney. "The Question of Recovery: An Introduction." *Social Text* 33, no. 4 (2015): 1–18.

Higginson, Thomas Wentworth. *Army Life in a Black Regiment*. 1869; New York: Norton, 1984.

Hollywood Reporter. "Nate Parker: 'I Felt Like This Was Something I Could Contribute to the Conversation.'" January 25, 2016. https://www.youtube.com /watch?v=6eSeq4Wbkyo.

Holt, Thomas. *The Problem of Freedom: Race, Labor, and Politics in Jamaica and Britain, 1832–1938*. Baltimore: Johns Hopkins University Press, 1991.

Hurston, Zora Neale. "Spirituals and Neo-Spirituals." In *Folklore, Memoirs, and Other Writings*, edited by Cheryl Wall, 869–74. New York: Library of America, 1995.

Hurston, Zora Neale. *Their Eyes Were Watching God*. 1937; New York: Harper Perennial, 2006.

Huyssen, Andreas. *Miniature Metropolis: Literature in an Age of Photography and Film*. Cambridge, MA: Harvard University Press, 2015.

Jacobs, Harriet. *Incidents in the Life of a Slave Girl*. 1861; New York: Library of America, 2001.

James, C. L. R. *Black Jacobins: Toussaint L'Ouverture and the San Domingo Revolution*. New York: Vintage, 1989.

Johnson, Clifton H. *God Struck Me Dead: Voices of Ex-Slaves*. New York: Pilgrim, 1969.

Johnson, James Weldon. "O Black and Unknown Bards." In *Writings*, edited by William Andrews, 817. New York: Library of America, 2004.

Johnson, James Weldon. "Preface: Book of Spirituals." In *Writings*, edited by William Andrews, 730–43. New York: Library of America, 2004.

Johnson, Walter. *River of Dark Dreams: Slavery and Empire in the Cotton Kingdom*. Cambridge, MA: Harvard University Press, 2013.

Johnson, Walter. *Soul by Soul: Life inside the Antebellum Slave Market*. Cambridge, MA: Harvard University Press, 1999.

Johnson, Walter. "White Lies: Human Property and Domestic Slavery aboard the Slave Ship *Creole*." *Atlantic Studies: Global Currents* 5, no. 2 (2008): 237–63.

Jones, Douglas. "Fruit of Abolition: Discontinuity and Difference in Terrence Hayes's 'The Avocado.'" In *The Psychic Hold of Slavery: Legacies in American*

Expressive Culture, edited by Aida Levy-Hussen, Soyica Diggs Colbert, and Robert Patterson, 39–54. New Brunswick, NJ: Rutgers University Press, 2016.

Jones, Edward P. *The Known World*. New York: Amistad, 2004.

Kazanjian, David. *The Brink of Freedom: Improvising Life in the Nineteenth-Century Atlantic World*. Durham, NC: Duke University Press, 2016.

Keizer, Arlene. *Black Subjects: Identity Formation in the Contemporary Narrative of Slavery*. Ithaca, NY: Cornell University Press, 2004.

King, Richard H. *Race, Culture, and the Intellectuals, 1940–1970*. Baltimore: Johns Hopkins University Press, 2004.

Kopytoff, Igor. "The Cultural Biography of Things: Commoditization as Process." In *The Social Life of Things: Commodities in Cultural Perspective*, edited by Arjun Appadurai, 64–91. Cambridge: Cambridge University Press, 1986.

Lane, Ann J., ed. *The Debate over Slavery: Stanley Elkins and His Critics*. Urbana: University of Illinois Press, 1973.

LeFlouria, Talitha L. *Chained in Silence: Black Women and Convict Labor in the New South*. Chapel Hill: University of North Carolina Press, 2015.

Levine, Lawrence. *Black Culture and Black Consciousness: Afro-American Folk Thought from Slavery to Freedom*. New York: Oxford University Press, 1977.

Levine, Robert S. *The Lives of Frederick Douglass*. Cambridge, MA: Harvard University Press, 2016.

Lincoln, C. Eric, and Lawrence H. Mamiya. *The Black Church in the African American Experience*. Durham, NC: Duke University Press, 1990.

Lott, Eric. *Love and Theft: Blackface Minstrelsy and the American Working Class*. New York: Oxford University Press, 1995.

Lovell, John, Jr. *Black Song: The Forge and the Flame; The Story of How the Afro-American Spiritual Was Hammered Out*. New York: Paragon 1972.

Madera, Judith. *Black Atlas: Geography and Flow in Nineteenth-Century African American Literature*. Durham, NC: Duke University Press, 2015.

Manigault-Bryant, LeRhonda S. *Talking to the Dead: Religion, Music, and Lived Memory among Gullah/Geechee Women*. Durham, NC: Duke University Press, 2014.

Marlowe, Christopher. *The Tragical History of Dr. Faustus*. 1604; London: Vizetelly, 1887.

Marriott, David. *Haunted Life: Visual Culture and Black Modernity*. New Brunswick, NJ: Rutgers University Press, 2007.

Martin, Jay. *Harvests of Change: American Literature, 1865–1914*. Englewood Cliffs, NJ: Prentice Hall, 1967.

McGruder, Aaron. "Return of the King." *The Boondocks*, season 1, episode 9 (2006).

McGruder, Aaron. "The Story of Catcher Freeman." *The Boondocks*, season 2, episode 12 (2008).

McKittrick, Katherine. *Demonic Grounds: Black Women and the Cartographies of Struggle*. Minneapolis: University of Minnesota Press, 2006.

McInnis, Maurie D. *Slaves Waiting for Sale: Abolitionist Art and the American Slave Trade*. Chicago: University of Chicago Press, 2011.

McMillan, Uri. *Embodied Avatars: Genealogies of Black Feminist Art and Performance*. New York: New York University Press, 2015.

Melville, Herman. "Benito Cereno." In *Piazza Tales and Other Prose Pieces*, 46–117. 1855; Evanston, IL: Northwestern University Press, 1987.

Michaels, Walter Benn. *Shape of the Signifier: 1967 to the End of History*. Princeton, NJ: Princeton University Press, 2004.

Mills, C. Wright. *The Power Elite: The American Middle Classes*. 1951; New York: Oxford University Press, 2002.

Mills, C. Wright, and Hans Gerth. *Character and Social Structure: The Psychology of Social Institutions*. 1953; New York: Harcourt Brace, 1964.

Mintz, Sidney W. *Caribbean Transformations*. New York: Columbia University Press, 1974.

Morrison, Toni. *Beloved*. 1987; New York: Vintage International Edition 2004.

Morrison, Toni. "City Limits, Village Values: Concepts of the Neighborhood in Black Fiction." In *Literature and the American Urban Experience: Essays on the City and Literature*, edited by Michael C. Jaye and Ann Chalmers Watts, 35–44. New Brunswick, NJ: Rutgers University Press, 1981.

Morrison, Toni. *Playing in the Dark: Whiteness and the Literary Imagination*. Cambridge, MA: Harvard University Press, 1992.

Moten, Fred. *In the Break: The Aesthetics of the Black Radical Tradition*. Minneapolis: University of Minnesota Press, 2003.

Moynihan, Daniel Patrick. *The Moynihan Report: The Negro Family—The Case for National Action*. 1965; New York: Cosimo Reports, 2018.

Murphy, Clifford R. "The Singing and Praying Bands of Maryland and Delaware." *Folkways*, fall/winter 2014. https://folkways.si.edu/magazine -fall-winter-2014-singing-praying-bands-maryland-delaware/gospel -african-american-sacred/music/article/smithsonian.

Murray, Albert. *The Omni-Americans: New Perspectives on Black Experience and American Culture*. New York: Outerbridge and Dientsfrey, 1970.

Myrdal, Gunnar. *An American Dilemma*. Vol. 1, *The Negro Problem and Modern Democracy*. London: Routledge, 1995.

Newman, Richard. *Go Down, Moses: Celebrating the African American Spiritual*. New York: Clarkson Potter, 1998.

NOLA.com. "Radcliffe Bailey's Stunning 'Windward Coast' at the CAC." March 4, 2015. https://www.youtube.com/watch?v=QUCo7YjvjXw.

Nyong'o, Tavia. *Afro-Fabulations: The Queer Drama of Black Life*. New York: New York University Press, 2019.

Olmsted, Frederick Law. *A Journey in the Seaboard Slave States*. New York: Dix and Edwards; Sampson Low, Son and Co., 1856.

Park, Robert E. *Race and Culture: Essays in the Sociology of Contemporary Man*. New York: Free Press, 1964.

Parker, Nate, dir. *The Birth of a Nation*. Century City, CA: Fox Searchlight Pictures, 2016.

Patterson, Orlando. *Freedom*. Vol. 1, *Freedom in the Making of Western Culture*. New York: Basic Books, 1991.

Patterson, Orlando. "The Peculiar Institution Again: *Roll, Jordan, Roll*." *New Republic*, November 9, 1974.

Patterson, Orlando. *Slavery and Social Death: A Comparative Study*. Cambridge, MA: Harvard University Press, 1982.

Phillips, Ulrich. *American Negro Slavery: A Survey of the Supply, Employment and Control of Negro Labor as Determined by the Plantation Regime*. New York: D. Appleton, 1918.

Posnock, Ross. *Philip Roth's Rude Truth: The Art of Immaturity*. Princeton, NJ: Princeton University Press, 2008.

Raboteau, Albert. *Slave Religion: The "Invisible Institution" in the Antebellum South*. New York: Oxford University Press, 1978.

Reagon, Bernice Johnson. Interview. *Bill Moyers Journal*, November 3, 2007. http://www.pbs.org/moyers/journal/11232007/profile3.html.

Reagon, Bernice Johnson. "The Songs Are Free." *Moyers on Democracy*, February 6, 1991. https://billmoyers.com/content/songs-free/.

Riesman, David, Nathan Glazer, and Reuel Denney. *The Lonely Crowd: A Study of the Changing American Character*. Garden City, NJ: Anchor, 1953.

Roberts, Neil. *Freedom as Marronage*. Chicago: University of Chicago Press, 2015.

Roth, Philip. *The Counterlife*. New York: Vintage, 1996.

Rusert, Britt. "Disappointment in the Archives of Black Freedom." *Social Text* 125, no. 4 (2015): 19–33.

Rusert, Britt. *Fugitive Science: Empiricism and Freedom in Early African American Culture*. New York: New York University Press, 2017.

Sambira, Jocelyne. "The Historic 'Ark of Return' Monument on Slavery Unveiled at the UN." United Nations, March, 25, 2015. https://www.un.org/africa renewal/web-features/historic-'ark-return'-monument-slavery-unveiled-un.

Scott, Daryl Michael. *Contempt and Pity: Social Policy and the Image of the Damaged Black Psyche, 1880–1996*. Chapel Hill: University of North Carolina Press, 1997.

Scott, David. *Conscripts of Modernity: The Tragedy of Colonial Enlightenment*. Durham, NC: Duke University Press, 2004.

Scott, David. *Stuart Hall's Voice: Intimations of an Ethics of Receptive Generosity*. Durham, NC: Duke University Press, 2017.

Seltzer, Mark. *Bodies and Machines*. London: Routledge, 1992.

Sharpe, Christina. *In the Wake: On Blackness and Being*. Durham, NC: Duke University Press, 2016.

Sharpe, Christina. *Monstrous Intimacies: Making Post-slavery Subjects*. Durham, NC: Duke University Press, 2010.

Smallwood, Stephanie E. *Saltwater Slavery: A Middle Passage from Africa to American Diaspora*. Cambridge, MA: Harvard University Press, 2009.

Snyder, Terri L. *The Power to Die: Slavery and Suicide in British North America*. Chicago: University of Chicago Press, 2015.

Spillers, Hortense J. *Black, White, and in Color: Essays on American Literature and Culture*. Chicago: University of Chicago Press, 2003.

Spillers, Hortense J. "Mama's Baby, Papa's Maybe: An American Grammar Book." In *Black, White, and in Color: Essays on American Literature and Culture*, 203–29. Chicago: University of Chicago Press, 2003.

Stampp, Kenneth. *The Peculiar Institution: Slavery in the Ante-bellum South*. New York: Knopf, 1956.

Stevenson, Brenda E. *Life in Black and White: Family and Community in the Slave South*. New York: Oxford University Press, 1996.

Stuckey, Sterling. *Slave Culture: Nationalist Theory and the Foundation of Black America*. New York: Oxford University Press, 1987.

Styron, William. *The Confessions of Nat Turner*. New York: Modern Library, 1967.

Sundquist, Eric. *To Wake the Nations: Race in the Making of American Literature*. Cambridge, MA: Harvard University Press, 1993.

Tannenbaum, Frank. *Slave and Citizen*. New York: Vintage, 1946.

Tarantino, Quentin. *Django Unchained*. Los Angeles: A Band Apart, 2012.

Tillet, Salamishah. *Sites of Slavery: Citizenship and Racial Democracy in the Post–Civil Rights Imagination*. Durham, NC: Duke University Press, 2012.

Trouillot, Michel-Rolph. "The Otherwise Modern: Caribbean Lessons from the Savage Slot." In *Critically Modern: Alternatives, Alterities, Anthropologies*, edited by Bruce Knauft, 220–37. Bloomington: Indiana University Press, 2002.

Trouillot, Michel-Rolph. *Silencing the Past: Power and the Production of History*. Boston: Beacon, 1995.

Turner, Nat. *The Confessions of Nat Turner, the Leader of the Late Insurrection in Southampton, Va.* Baltimore: Lucas & Deaver, 1831.

Wagner, Bryan. *Disturbing the Peace: Black Culture and the Police Power after Slavery*. Cambridge, MA: Harvard University Press, 2009.

Warren, Kenneth W. *So Black and Blue: Ralph Ellison and the Occasion of Criticism*. Chicago: University of Chicago Press, 2003.

Weber, Max. *The Protestant Ethic and the Spirit of Capitalism*. Translated by Talcott Parsons. London: Routledge, 1992.

Weheliye, Alexander G. *Habeas Viscus: Racializing Assemblages, Biopolitics, and Black Feminist Theories of the Human*. Durham NC: Duke University Press, 2014.

White, Deborah Gray. *Ar'n't I a Woman? Female Slaves in the Plantation South.* New York: Norton, 1999.

Whyte, William H. *The Organization Man.* Philadelphia: University of Pennsylvania Press, 2002.

Wilderson, Frank B., III. *Red, White and Black: Cinema and the Structure of U.S. Antagonisms.* Durham, NC: Duke University Press, 2010.

Williams, Heather Andrea. *Self-Taught: African American Education in Slavery and Freedom.* Chapel Hill: University of North Carolina Press, 2005.

Wilson, Edmund. *Patriotic Gore: Studies in the Literature of the American Civil War.* New York: Farrar, Straus and Giroux, 1962.

Wilson, Ivy G. *Specters of Democracy: Blackness and the Aesthetics of Politics in the Antebellum U.S.* New York: Oxford University Press, 2011.

Wood, Peter. *Black Majority: Negroes in Colonial South Carolina from 1670 through the Stono Rebellion.* New York: Norton, 1974.

Wong, Edlie L. *Neither Fugitive nor Free.* New York: New York University Press, 2009.

Wright, Richard. "How Bigger Was Born." In *Native Son*, 431–62. 1940; New York: Harper Perennial, 1993.

Wright, Richard. *Twelve Million Black Voices.* New York: Thunder's Mouth Press, 1941.

Young, Kevin. *The Grey Album: On the Blackness of Blackness.* Minneapolis: Graywolf Press, 2012.